MARTHA RODMAN

FAITH
ENCOUNTERS

Learning to Walk with Jesus Daily

TABLE OF CONTENTS

FORWARD

Martha and her late husband, Darryl Rodman, came into my life during a season of needed counsel, a season shortly before receiving the lead pastoral role at Life Church in Oak Harbor, Washington. While Darryl initially was the primary voice of wisdom in my life during that season, we would shortly discover that Martha would be a wise counselor and encourager to my wife and me soon after Darryl's major stroke. Like Darryl, Martha's experience included bi-coastal ministry. In addition, they held an apostolic voice to many churches, offering encouragement, counsel, leadership, prophetic ministry, worship, women's ministry, marriage counseling, and seminars. Martha, to this day, continues to provide many of these strengths to the body of Christ in many churches. Specifically, within our church, her contributions continue to abound in many needed leadership roles.

Martha's life has been a journey of walking out her faith with Jesus, and I believe this book to be a great invitation to a deeper faith walk with Him. Martha's open, honest, and transparent style invites the reader to identify with the everyday struggles we all face but quickly offers a better way, an invitation, to walk it out in faith. I encourage you to read this book with an open heart and mind, and allow yourself to be inspired as you respond to the invitation to pray at the closing of each chapter.

Michael Hurley

Lead Pastor Life Church

Ministers Fellowship International - ALT Board Member

PREFACE

Life is full of challenges. Thankfully God's word can teach us how to stand upright and help carry each other through them. Faith Encounters can occur as we are reading scripture, problem solving through prayer or even through the counsel of others. The personal stories you will read in the following pages exemplify God's grace, mercy and help during my own time of need or struggles. Some were lessons of needed correction! Most were God's love made manifest through His love and grace. What a privilege it is to walk with the Creator of the Universe. It is my hope that these faith encounters will encourage you to re-affirm yours or seek Him for more.

It is my prayer that you will be encouraged to know Him, love Him and serve Him because He is so worthy. Keep walking my friend. Keep walking.

May God Bless You and Keep You.

Martha Rodman

1.

Faith and Remembering Who You Are With

Little children, you are from God and have overcome them,
for he who is in you is greater than he who is in the world.
I John 4:4 ESV

Today is a great day to remember that you are not alone. It is a day to remind yourself that he who is in you is greater than he who is in the world, 1 John 4:4. Sometimes, even when we 'know' this truth, we need to deliberately bring it to the forefront of our minds and remember WHO it is that is in you and with you. It is also a day of remembering he is Lord.

He is the God who created the universe, and he holds **your** world as well.

He is the God who listens to the bird's song, and **your** heart's cry as well.

He is the God who sees your struggles and says I am **your** strength.

He is the God who from the beginning of time has had a plan for the world, and that includes **your** life as well.

He is the God who spoke and the world was formed and He's given **you** a voice to join his words to bring change to your world.

He is the God who is always present, even when **you** feel alone.

He is God, even in the shadows of death or fear**, you** are not alone.

He is the God of all Hope, even when **you** feel hopeless.

He is the healer of broken hearts and broken dreams, he is **your** restorer.

He sent Jesus His Son to save His people from their sin, which includes **you**!

He is the Lord of lords, the King of kings. Let him reign today in **your** life.

He is a Faithful God, and he is faithful to **you.**

Friends, 2 Chronicles tells the story of Asa, King of Judah who faced an army of Ethiopians. Asa had 300,000 warriors and Zerah, the Ethiopian had 1,000,000, yes 1 million men fighting against Judah. Asa cried out to the Lord, *"O Lord, no one but you can help the powerless against the mighty! Help us, O Lord for we trust in you alone. It is in your name that we have come against this vast horde. O Lord, you are our God, do not let mere men prevail against you! So the Lord defeated the Ethiopians in the presence of Asa and the army of Judah and the enemy fled. 2 Chronicles 14:11-12 ESV.*

Asa could have simply surrendered, but he remembered the Lord His God and they were victorious. Later on in chapter 15, Azariah, a prophet spoke to Asa and said; *Listen, all you people of Judah and Benjamin! The Lord will stay with you as long as you stay with him! Whenever you seek him, you will find him. But if you abandon him, he will abandon* you. Verse 5 goes on to say, *"During those dark times, it was not safe to travel. Problems troubled the people of every land. Nation fought against nation and city against city, for God was troubling them with every kind of problem. But as for you, be strong and courageous, for your work will be rewarded. When Asa heard this message from Azariah the prophet, he took courage and removed all the detestable idols from the land of Judah and Benjamin..."*

Today we are facing many troubles in nations all over the world. I think the troubles we are facing stem from God allowing us as nations to do our own sin thing. It is time to remember whose we are and allow him to be Lord of our life, he will show us the way through with victory and strength. It is a time to remember him and his ways. It is time to not only remember he is Lord but allow him to be **your Lord**.

Father, I thank you for reminding us that You are Sovereign. Remind us that we are yours and you are ours. We choose to submit to you and your ways, trusting you know what is best. Thank you that you are working all things together for our good.

In Jesus' Name, amen.

2.

Faith and Dry Bones

..."Son of man, can these bones live?"...
Ezekiel 37:3 ESV

My Bible reading program brought me to Ezekiel 37 this week. As I began to read about God's famous question to Ezekiel, "Can these bones live?" I felt the Holy Spirit ask me the same thing. It was like a jolt. Faith began to arise and I began to look around at the things in my life that I have just accepted as being dry and done. No life. No faith. Just acceptance of the way it is, so it stayed.

As the question to Ezekiel became *my* question, I began to get excited. I began to ask him to show me what areas in my life I had just accepted the circumstances. To my surprise, he showed me my health. It has been especially difficult for the past few months. I went to the doctor, and after testing, I found out my thyroid was not doing its job. So I started on thyroid meds, but then, I experienced an asthma flair and I could hardly walk across the room without experiencing shortness of breath. I began to pray specifically about these two issues.

Monday morning, I woke to a shift in the circumstances. I could actually get things done! I believe the allergies and asthma are coming subject to his word as well. My breathing will come alive and I can do what he calls me to do. The drying bones of my lungs are coming to life.

My friends, what or where are your dry bones? Is it in your marriage relationship? Your job situation? Your finances? Your life perspectives? Your health? Hopelessness? Maybe you have some bones in your life that seem to be 'drying and dying'. Don't wait until they are dead! Begin to speak life into them in the Name of Jesus. Hopeless situations do not have to stay hopeless. We serve an amazing Savior that came into this world with power and might that he wants to impart into us, for us.

Ezekiel's response was, "O Lord GOD, only you know," Ezekiel 37:3 ESV. We can read that with a sense of resignation, or we can let it begin to kindle expectation. Your thoughts may have settled on a belief that if God wanted to change things, they would change. However, he used Ezekiel to prophesy to those bones. He spoke to the dead bones while they were yet dead. He spoke in faithful obedience, as we should.

Maybe your dry bones are in the area of your parenting. Your child is a struggling learner. Do not lose hope. Begin to speak faith and encouragement to them. Call for the breakthroughs needed. Maybe you feel like it is your patience that is dry and dead. Remember, we have the fruit of the Holy Spirit working within. Ask him for insight and direction.

When you begin to speak where his Spirit is prompting, release your faith and expect change. Do not let fear paralyze you from speaking to those hard or dry things. Expect change to happen. Lift your voice and declare life, not death. I have experienced Godly intervention, and you can too. He is good.

"Can these dry bones live?" I am excited as I sense breakthroughs coming despite past experiences, your dry bones can and will live. It may take time. It may take tenacity, but they will live.

Father, I speak life to every 'dry bone' area in our lives. We thank you for your power being released in those areas. We choose to water them with faith and Your Word.

In Jesus' Name, amen.

3.

Faith and Thoughts on Psalm 62

I wait quietly before God, for my victory comes from him.
Psalm 62:1 NLT

I love this Psalm.

I am learning to wait quietly with him. I've chosen to slow down my devotional time with him, and it has brought a fresh peace and blessing to my spirit. Psalm 62:1-2 in The Passion Translation says: *I stand silently to listen for the one I love, waiting as long as it takes for the Lord to rescue me. For God alone has become my Savior. He alone is my safe place.* In our busy scary world, where is your safe place? Can I remind you today that we have one? We have a safe place we can escape to.

David wrote this psalm while he was in trouble. As we read on, we see he is very clear that he is being hunted by his enemies. What did he do? He encouraged himself in the Lord. Do you feel oppressed, depressed, and discouraged today? Go to the Lord. As Louie Giglio has said, learn to linger longer in His presence. Let the Lord begin to speak to you of His help and hope. The Passion Translation goes on in verse 2, *"He alone is my safe place;* **his wrap-around presence always protects me.** *For he is my champion defender; there's no risk of failure with God. So why would I let worry paralyze me, even when troubles multiply around me?"* My question to you and me is, "why would I let worry paralyze me into inaction and fear?" We don't have to. As we wait quietly for His assurance, he comes with hope and grace.

Verse 5-8 in the NLT says, *"Let all that I am wait quietly before God, for my hope is in him. He alone is my rock and my salvation, my fortress, where I will not be shaken. My victory and honor come from God alone. He is my refuge, a rock where no enemy can reach me. Oh my people, trust in him at all times. Pour out your heart to him, for God is our refuge."* I encourage you today to trust in him. Take the time to pour out your heart to him, not just carry the worry and anxiety around with you. Write it down if you need to. When we take the time to pray and unload our cares to him, we find life is easier to manage. Cast them upon him for he cares. Do not let the enemy lie to you and tell you it won't make a difference. Release your faith and try it.

It worked for King David, and it will work for you. The New King James translation says it this way: *Trust in Him at all times, ye people; pour out your heart before Him; God is a refuge for us.* Psalm 62:8. It's all-inclusive. No one is left out, including you. He hears you. He sees you. He longs to be that refuge for you. Ask him to teach you how to find refuge in him. He longs to show you. He is available right now to be your shelter in the time of any storm. Go to him.

Father, I thank you that you are always listening to us. You are our safe place. Teach us to run to you sooner, rather than later. To linger longer with you so we can regain strength, hope, and discover your ways through any wilderness we may be facing. We choose to trust you today, knowing we are secure in your Presence.

In Jesus' Name, amen.

4.

Faith to Surrender

"...Because of the joy awaiting him, he endured the cross, disregarding its shame..." Hebrews 12:2 NLT

Early Sunday morning as I was driving to our Easter service, I began thinking about the faith it takes to surrender to the Lord and his will for our lives. I realized we would not be celebrating Easter if Jesus had not surrendered to his Father's will of the death on the cross. He is our wonderful example.

The faith that is involved in surrendering to his will is not easy. Hebrews 12:2 b *NLT says, "Because of the joy awaiting him, he endured the cross, disregarding its shame."* The NKJV says, *"who for the joy that was set before him endured the cross, despising the shame, and has sat down at the right hand of the throne of God."* Jesus thought about what he was going to have to endure. I always wonder how he went from the last meal with his disciples, where he served them; lovingly washing their feet, sharing what we now call communion with them, all the while knowing what was coming when he released Judas to his mission of betrayal. They then made the trip to the Garden of Gethsemane. Have you ever brought people who you know care about you into a situation and asked them to pray or stand with you, but had them fall short of what you thought you needed them to do? Jesus implored his friends to pray with him, but they fell short. His prophetic words to Peter about his upcoming denial must have added to his pain.

Two aspects of that scripture in Hebrews stand out to me. He endured the cross and he disregarded its shame. We are not asked to be crucified on a cross, we are asked to carry it. That can bring shame as well. Our culture is not pro-cross carriers in the United States, but we are called to carry it anyway. We do it for the joy that is set before us.

Still, Jesus pressed on. We won't be asked to endure the cross and have the sins of the world upon us, but at times we are asked to surrender to what may feel unfair or impossible. Years ago, Darryl and I were scheduled to take our two children on a road trip to Rhode Island from Idaho. We prepped and planned, believing God would send us money to make the trip. We were pioneering a small church and were able to live and pay our bills each month, but did not have any extra for the trip. Darryl built some beds in our VW van as we planned on sleeping in it to avoid motel expenses.

As the day of departure drew near, we still didn't have the extra funds. I remember my husband declaring, "Satan, we will leave here. God will make a way and that is that." It seemed foolish and silly to set out on a 2000-mile trip with little funds. Long story short, we left Idaho with about $40 and ended up in Rhode Island with $50. There were many difficult adventures on that trip, but we made it. We left on the trip with God's Word of Faith in our hearts and a complete peace knowing we were being obedient to His will. We chose obedience despite what we saw or had in our pockets and God opened the door to relationships we still enjoy and affect to this day.

I am not comparing what Jesus obediently endured on the same level as that story at all. I am encouraging us to listen to His voice and trust him, even when it seems impossible. Sometimes faith surrendered means you do things 'on the quiet', where nobody knows it was you. No glamor, no glory, just a quiet step of obedience that will bring blessings from him.

Laying up treasure in heaven doesn't always manifest itself on earth. Sometimes, faith surrendered means you humble yourself and put someone else ahead of you. Last month I said Yes to the Lord in supporting a ministry in New England on a monthly basis, rather than giving from time to time. It was a faith step I wanted to make but seemed difficult financially. I committed and God has been surprising me with some amazing extra gifts to Impart Ministries. No one knew of my commitment but me, Jesus, and the ministry. He is faithful.

Sometimes surrendering our faith means we bear with things we don't like. Paul had his thorn in the flesh. I am living without my Darryl. His stroke happened many years ago, but I am still surrendering to God's will in this area. There is nothing I can do about changing it, but I find myself still struggling at times. Then I pray for his grace and ask him to use me, teach me, help me, and make the most out of this difficult time for his purpose and his glory. I see his fruitfulness in my life. As I read about Jesus' struggle in the Garden, I understand that he understands, which is comforting and encouraging. Surrendering to his will is always best, but not always easy.

Father, I ask you to give us a fresh perspective on how You see our trials and difficulties. I thank you for helping us to walk in surrendered faith each day, trusting your will and your way is always best. Not only for me but others around me also. Thank you, dear Father, for your grace and mercy in this area.

In Jesus' Name, amen.

5.

Faith and Always

"I know the Lord is always with me. I will not be shaken,
for he is right beside me." Psalm 16:8 NLT

I have lost count of how many times newscasters, pastors, and others have used the phrase, 'in these unprecedented times,' during difficult seasons. It means, 'never done or known before,' and it is true, we as global citizens have never lived in such a season as this. So many unknowns and upheavals to our normal life are very unsettling. Political issues, vaccinated versus unvaccinated, masked versus unmasked, fueling controversies and divisions across the world. It has led me to wonder, what is stable? What can I believe in?

I came across this small little word the other day as I was doing my Bible study. The word always–at all times, forever. As I meditated on it, it was so comforting.

I know the Lord is always with me, I will not be shaken, for he is right beside me. Psalm 16:8 NLT

But you are always the same; you will live forever. The children of your people will live in security. Their children's children will thrive in your presence. Psalm 102:27-28 NLT

I am with you always, even to the end of the age. Matthew 28:20b NLT

These scriptures are so comforting. We can depend on them. We can go back to them for stability when we are shaken. Believers, remember there are also some strong instructions given to us about, 'always'. These are admonitions that if followed, will advance the kingdom of God, not only in our lives but in the lives of others. I know we think, "I can't *always* be consistent," but we can certainly try!

I will always trust in God's unfailing love. I will choose, no matter what my circumstances look like, to trust in his love for me. I will silence the voices in my head that tell me the opposite, for he has proven his love through Calvary.

There is joy for those who deal justly with others and always do what is right. Psalm 106:3 NLT

Please understand this is not done in our own strength, but by the power of the Holy Spirit. It is a mindset where we choose to live our lives with the Fruit of the Spirit flowing out of our hearts. We do what is right because of his righteousness, not our own. In fact, we're not always sure of what is right without his wisdom! Setting our minds and hearts on doing the right thing even when it seems to be to our harm is a by-product of our trust in his love.

Instead, you must worship Christ as the Lord of your life. And if someone asks about your hope as a believer, always be ready to explain it. But do this in a gentle and respectful way. 1 Peter 3:15-16a NLT

This takes some preparation. I read in Acts 7 the other day that Stephen was arrested and taken before the council to defend himself.

Two thoughts struck me as I read his response, a lengthy discourse of Israel's history in 52 verses to the leaders. This man knew his stuff! Called to be one of the first deacons; we know he met the qualifications of being well-respected and full of the Spirit and wisdom. He was prepared.

Fear, intimidation, and insecurity grow when we feel unprepared. Stephen knew how to rely on the Holy Spirit. He learned to trust him to fill his mouth! We as believers, need to learn how to rely on him to word our mouths during difficult times, but it comes with practice. If you struggle with talking to different types of people or in different situations, study 2 Timothy 2:15 AMP, *"Study and be eager and do your utmost to present yourself to God approved (tested by trial), a workman who has no cause to be ashamed, correctly analyzing and accurately dividing [rightly handling and skillfully teaching] the Word of Truth."*

This means that we as believers can choose to grow up in him. We put off childish excuses, "I can't, I don't know how, I'm not smart enough," and we make the choice to learn. We have the best teacher, the Holy Spirit who longs to come alongside us to strengthen, teach and enable us.

As you read through the Bible, take note of the word 'always'. What a comfort it is to know God is always with us, helping, strengthening, convicting, and changing us to be more like him.

Thank you, Father, for helping us to become more like you. Remind us that you are always with us. You are always the same trustworthy Father, that we can depend on. Help us to model your faithfulness.

In Jesus' Name, Amen.

6.

Faith and Denying Yourself

Then Jesus told his disciples, "If anyone would come after me,
let him deny himself and take up his cross and follow me."
Matthew 16:24 ESV

After years of following the Lord, I know that His ways are best. A 'yes' often leads to unexpected changes, but he is always trustworthy. When our girls were two and 6 months old, God directed us to take a road trip to the east coast. The plan was to connect with our ministry partners and attend a wedding of a longtime friend. Two weeks of adventures!

A few days after our arrival we went to Massachusetts, to attend the wedding. On the way to the wedding, we stopped at another ministry home. As we walked into the house I heard in my spirit Satan laughing and cackling, "Some ministry house this is," It was a shock to me and I found myself replying to his taunts saying, "God, I don't care what you have to do, shut him up, Lord." I found out later that the current leaders were struggling with marriage issues and other attacks which led them to seek some unwise choices influenced by our enemy.

As I stood there in the foyer hearing those taunts, and as I responded to those taunts with that phrase, 'no matter what it takes,' I did not know the course of change I was setting in motion. The following day our overseer asked Darryl and me if we would move into that home and take over the pastorate! This was not what I expected. I already felt awkward and confused by some of the obvious differences between the west and the east–but I had asked the Lord to make the changes, so what choice did I have? If you are upset about something–be prepared to be the solution!

Talk about denying my flesh and wants–this was not on our agenda. We had planned to be gone for two weeks and now we were being asked to remain for an unspecified time! As we discussed what would happen to our home and church in Idaho and what it would mean for the church and ministry in Massachusetts, we felt God say 'yes' we should stay. He would work all those other things out.

None of it was easy. It became a learning school for us in so many ways. The Holy Spirit began to teach me some very interesting lessons. Such as us often thinking the familiar is always 'better' than the 'new'. I found myself comparing the west coast to the east coast, and due to this prejudice, the west coast always seemed better. I finally learned, that different is just different and to stop putting a judgment on certain things which was a great lesson to have learned when we did ministry overseas! I learned that spiritual warfare is real. For months I had to remind myself every day that putting on the helmet of salvation was not an option! To defeat and silence that voice took perseverance and determination.

I learned about homesickness, and how to give it to the Lord. It has given me compassion for the many military folks we've encountered here in Washington. I learned that God loves and cares for our nation and he loves diversity. As the years passed and we traveled back and forth from the east to the west, I learned to appreciate the different aspects of our nation. Yes, we had to 'deny ourselves' to live in a new place, learning new ways and new things—but it was worth it. We made longtime friends and it opened doors of ministry and influence that we still have today.

We discussed in our Life Group the other day what denying yourself meant versus self-denial. Someone described it this way, self-denial is our decision to refrain from something, while denying ourselves for the gospel's sake is submitting to God's request. There is no way we can take up our cross and follow him without first recognizing the focus is His will, not our will. Learning to trust His will as the better way takes doing it! As we practice his will every day, it becomes easier to say yes. I still struggle from time to time, but I have learned that His way really is the better way. It is not always the easy or painless way, but we can trust it will bring good fruit. I love and miss my east coast brethren. My life is so much richer because of them. The lessons were hard, but the fruit is sweeter. Please say yes to him. You won't regret it.

*Father, I thank you for **your will**. I thank you for helping us learn to say "yes" to you, even when it is difficult. I thank you that you did not shy away from the cross. I ask that you give us the grace to take up our cross to follow you, no matter where it may lead or what it may cost.*

In Jesus' Name, Amen.

7.

Faith and God's Action Words

Listen to me, all who hope for deliverance—all who seek the Lord!
Isaiah 51:1 NLT

The Holy Spirit caught my attention while reading through the book of Isaiah. Do you know how many special action words Isaiah uses in talking to the Israelites and to us? Well, I confess I don't either! I know God's action words are throughout the Bible, but they caught my attention in Isaiah.

Actions words like 'listen'. *Listen to me, all who hope for deliverance—all who seek the Lord! Consider the rock from which you were cut, the quarry from which you were mined. Isaiah 51:1 NLT.*

Listen to me, you who know right from wrong, you who cherish my law in your hearts. Do not be afraid of people's scorn, nor fear their insults. Isaiah 51:7 NLT

I felt like a child whose parent was trying their best to get their attention. While homeschooling my grandchildren, I often tell them 'listen up'. This is important. I feel God is trying not only to get my attention but the attention of his church. We need to listen much more attentively than ever before. We must remember who it is that is speaking to us. It is the Lord of Heaven and Earth. My Lord, who has my best interest at heart. It is your Savior, who loves you more than anything.

I am trying to practice listening. Sunday morning I knew it was going to be a long morning, so I went to make coffee in my travel cup. It is something I often do, especially if I serve both services. Quietly I heard the Lord say, "Not today." Instead of arguing and pondering His reasons, I just walked away from the coffeemaker empty-handed. I trusted he had His reason. I congratulated myself on listening! I think listening begs the question, "Are we using the ears he has given us to hear?"

I watch my children teach their children the importance of listening during dangerous times. Little ones don't always know why they need to stop when mom says stop, but they learn to trust her voice. I hope to learn to trust His voice even more. I need to become a better listener.

Another 'action word' that caught my attention is wake up. Wake up or awake! Isaiah 51:17-19 NLT is very sobering. *Wake up, wake up, O Jerusalem! You have drunk the cup of the Lord's fury. You have drunk the cup of terror, tipping out its last drops. Not one of your children is left alive to take your hand and guide you. These two calamities have fallen on you: desolation and destruction, famine and war. And who is left to sympathize with you? Who is left to comfort you?*

Terrible things had happened to them and, in a way, they didn't even understand or realize it. Is that what is happening in our culture? Are we so asleep that we are losing the next generation to destructive and desolate thoughts and actions that are definitely against the Word of God? We need to wake up with courage and faith. We need to arise with hope and be about our Father's business.

Wake up, wake up, O Zion! Clothe yourself with strength. Put on your beautiful clothes, O holy city of Jerusalem, for unclean and godless people will enter your gates no longer. Rise from the dust, O Jerusalem. Sit in a place of honor. Remove the chains of slavery from your neck, O captive daughter of Zion, Isaiah 52:1-2 NLT.

Let us wake up and listen to His Words. Let us put on His strength, learning to lean on him and His wisdom. These two action words, 'listen and wake' are for each of us, as His children.

Father, I ask you to help us wake up and listen. I ask that as we read your Word, we put into action your requests. I thank you for opening our ears so that we may hear your direction and assignment. We are called to be your lights in this dark world, help make it so. Forgive us for sleeping on the job. Help us to pray for our leaders, both spiritual and governmental, during these difficult days.

In Jesus' Name. Amen

8.

Faith and Surprises

I no longer call you slaves, because a master doesn't confide in his slaves. Now you are my friends since I have told you everything the Father told me. John 15:15 NLT

About 12 years ago or so we needed a new fridge. One of the features I wanted was an ice maker. In our previous fridge, there was the option to have one, but my husband did not want to have to worry about getting the water pipe to it—concerned about possible leaks, etc. So we opted out. I persisted in my wishes when we needed to purchase a new fridge and it not only came with the ice maker installed—he paid a friend to install the water line for me! I felt so loved and excited to finally have this great feature of an ice maker.

It has been so fun to simply open the freezer compartment and have fresh ice whenever I want to without the struggle of filling and refilling ice trays. I have so enjoyed this feature. I know many people have fridges that dispense water, ice cubes, and crushed ice on the front of their fridge. Even though we could have chosen one of those options, we did not. I was one happy camper just getting the ice cube maker! (It still makes me happy!)

A few months ago, I noticed a light inside my fridge had turned from green to red. I thought, what does this mean? The notice by it mentioned something about it being time to change the filter. I hunted all around for something to remove/replace it but I couldn't find anything so I just sort of ignored it while praying it wasn't hurting anything!

A few weeks ago, as we were cleaning out the fridge I noticed a button. I pushed said button and water came out!! Not only did I have an ice maker all these years, but I also had a cold water dispenser inside my fridge! Talk about a surprise! For 12 years I lived unaware of this amazing feature that we bought. I know it is hard to believe that I did not notice this feature—but because I am tall and the button is hidden under a dip in the freezer door it was harder to notice. When I clean my fridge I am looking inside—usually on my hands and knees and don't look up!

I realized that my excitement and enthusiasm for my ice maker made me content with that feature, so I did not even think to explore other features. I think that is how it can be with the Lord; we get excited about one aspect of our walk with him and miss some of his 'other' benefits. We enjoy salvation and the forgiveness of our sins, but we may not embrace the power he has given us through the Holy Spirit. We partake in our personal walk with him, but neglect to connect with his family through the local church. We enjoy reading the comfort of the Psalms but do not explore some of the 'meatier' passages encouraging us to walk and live holy through the New Testament.

My grandchildren are now enjoying this new feature as well. I felt so foolish to not have seen this, now obvious, feature for all these years, but I am excited and blessed to have easy access to cold filtered water at the push of a button. I asked the Lord to show me things I have been missing or overlooking in my walk with him. I find myself praying more for myself and others. As I pray he has caused a greater appreciation for the gifts others have that I may have overlooked before. In some ways, I feel like He has given me better sight!

Father, I thank you for opening our eyes to Your surprises. Help us to see **you** *in others. To appropriate more of you in our lives and help impart it to others. Just like the fresh cold water tap was available to me for twelve years and I was ignorant of it, help me to receive your insight into other blind areas in my life that I may reflect your character and glory even more.*

In Jesus' Name, amen.

9.

Faith and Challenges: When Life Gets Real

Don't worry about anything; instead, pray about everything.
Tell God what you need and thank him for all he has done.
Then you will experience God's peace, which exceeds anything we
can understand. His peace will guard your hearts and minds as you
live in Christ Jesus. Philippians 4:6-7 NLT

What would life look like if we truly walked in faith in our everyday life circumstances? Each day presents us with dozens of opportunities to activate our faith. God has been taking me deeper in this area than ever before. Scripture says, *"So then faith comes by hearing, and hearing by the Word of God,"* Romans 10:17 NKJV. When I am challenged by life circumstances, like health issues, financial obstacles, or relationship struggles, do I turn to God's Word or do I sit in my own thoughts?

"*Gracious words are like a honeycomb, sweetness to the soul and health to the body,"* Proverbs 16:24 ESV.

"And my God shall supply all your need according to His riches in glory by Christ Jesus," Philippians 4:19 NKJV.

"Be completely humble and gentle; be patient, bearing with one another in love. Make every effort to keep the unity of the Spirit through the bond of peace," Ephesians 4:2-3 NIV.

So how do we apply faith when dealing with situations that have unknown or potentially unwelcomed outcomes?

Once I accompanied a loved one to the hospital to have a diagnostic CT scan trying to find the source of their discomfort. The physician assistant requested the scan expecting to find some Diverticulitis. However, after the scan was finished, we were requested to return immediately to the medical clinic. As we rode back to the clinic I prayed that no matter what the diagnosis was, it was under the name of Jesus. The concern did not reign over the name of Jesus. I activated my faith in the face of the unknown.

As we waited in the waiting room, peace still prevailed. I could tell my dear one was not feeling well. They ushered us back and informed us there was a mass in the abdomen looking like the pancreas, spleen, and abdomen were involved. Later testing revealed it was a 10 cm tumor. I quietly said, "It's going to be ok, God has a plan." The PA asked if the patient prayed and when she said yes, she asked if she could pray for us! As we held hands and she prayed, we felt the presence of God and we continued to walk in His peace. Together we activated our faith in the middle of the unknown.

There was a lot to process and absorb. We drove to her house and shared the news with her husband. You can imagine the shock and disbelief along with many hugs and reassurances as we shared the situation with him. I left them and went home to make some phone calls and do some processing myself.

The next morning, God led me to Philippians 4:6-7 NLT. I knew this was his strategy to help me in situations like this. It was not a new revelation, but it was so clear to me that as I employ its strategy, peace prevails and faith keeps us firmly on the path of God's peace and wisdom.

Dear Friend, you might want to read this next scripture aloud. *Don't worry about anything; instead, pray about everything. Tell God what you need, and thank him for all he has done. Then you will experience God's peace, which exceeds anything we can understand. His peace will guard your hearts and minds as you live in Christ Jesus, Philippians 4:6-7 NLT.*

How do we practically do this daily, in the face of challenges big and small?

Step 1: *Don't worry about anything.* Wow, this can be a tough one. I realize I need to capture those stray fear thoughts, those, "what if," thoughts, and the, "but what about this," type of thoughts. Our first challenge was not to go, "OH NO! the pancreas is involved, and the survival rate of pancreatic cancer is not good." I had to take my mind off those statistics and put them on the God who reigns over everything. We had no sure diagnosis at that time. So, I chose not to let my mind go to the worst-case scenario. It took effort, but as I reminded myself we don't know the diagnosis, so I chose to do the next step as we waited for the test results.

Step 2: *Pray about everything.* Instead of worrying, pray. Capture those rogue fear thoughts with prayer. Talk to him about your fears and concerns. I was reminded again of the blessing of having the Holy Spirit as my prayer partner! He loves those involved. After Starla, the PA's prayer I added one of my own, "God, get every good thing you can out of this because you know this is hard. Use it for your good. In Jesus Name, amen."

Step 3: *Tell God what you need.* Scripture exhorts us not to borrow trouble from tomorrow, but to live each day with trust in him. So every day, I asked him for the grace for the day and His direction specifically needed for this situation. Clear diagnosis, wisdom for which hospital, doctors, pain and nausea control, good communication, and rest are some of the prayers we prayed. Peace for family members who were struggling with fear was a big one. Taking one bite at a time this elephant will be walked out. (A mixed metaphor I know!)

Step 4: *Thank him for all he has done.* We have already seen His hand in this situation. We thanked him for sunny days and his love for us. Cultivating thankfulness during stressful times is a tool for maintaining faith and grace in the situation. It is a great reminder of who we are placing our faith in and what he can and will do. He has not and will not leave us in our trials by ourselves, but he comes into the midst with his presence.

Step 5: *Then you will experience God's peace, which exceeds everything we can understand.* We cannot try to figure out everything right now. The 'whys' are a big detractor during stressful challenges. This is not the time to try to figure everything out. Walk in the peace he gives and rest in that. Cast the other concerns on him and watch His hand move.

Step 6: *His peace will guard your hearts and minds as you live in Christ Jesus.* We need to let his peace guard our hearts and our minds. Otherwise, they will be assaulted with tormenting fears and all the worst-case scenarios. Most will never happen. Those thoughts rob us of the gift of our today. I believe we are going to continue to see God's hand moving and I trust this child of God will enjoy long days on this earth. However, there are times when our natural best-case scenario doesn't happen and perhaps our loved ones are taken home. God is still in control and still moving his good purpose and will. Just as in everything else, do not let the enemy of your soul steal the gift of the present with those you love.

These steps work in the big trials of life, and the small ones. As we apply Philippians 4:6-7, we will walk in His peace. When we walk in His peace, we are more able to help others in their struggles.

Father, I thank you that you are helping us learn that we do not need to worry; that we can talk to you about everything, and then we will experience your peace. As the days grow darker, we will need to become very familiar with these steps, not only for ourselves but for others. Help me Lord, to apply your wonderful word and its promises to every situation I face.

In Jesus' Name, amen.

10.

Faith and the New Normal

The Lord is near to the brokenhearted and saves
the crushed in spirit. Psalm 34:18 ESV

Oftentimes, as December is drawing to a close, I use it as a season of reflection. This season of reflection allows me to take stock, measure change, celebrate wins, and realize losses as I say goodbye to one year and prepare to embrace a new one. Some years bring about more intense change than others.

Some shifts are expected. Many are not. Not all are considered bad. Many are welcomed. A wedding, new baby, job promotion, or planned retirement all have many wonderful blessings embedded in them. I consider these changes, the 'planned new normal'. These are opportunities that most people celebrate. A chosen shift.

Unfortunately, others had their 'new normal' thrust upon them without their permission. The fifty-eight killed and 489 injured in the senseless shootings in Las Vegas, Nevada in 2017 had their worlds invaded by pain and loss. They must deal with their 'new normal'. No options. Unexpected life-altering diagnoses, infidelity discoveries, miscarriages, or even unplanned pregnancies can't help but impact normal life.

My world totally shifted in 2010 when my beloved husband, Darryl Rodman, suffered a major stroke. So many shifts took place in an instant. I went from a wife--supporting my husband and partnering in our ministry together to making all the decisions. Suddenly I was a caregiver, and in all ways practical, the head of our home.

As I sought stability and God's perspective, I kept hearing, 'accept this new normal in your life'. Then in 2012, my world shifted again as I went from wife to widow. Another new normal to accept. Another year. Another shift. I honestly struggled to accept my new normal first, as a caregiver then as a widow. Believe me, it was a fierce struggle at times

As a shifting event takes place, often in a single moment, the processing of it in our soul and spirit takes much longer. This past Saturday, I learned about a young woman in our church who is facing her shocking new normal as her husband and the father of their young son passed away unexpectedly. Another friend stopped by this week to share with me how the experimental chemo treatments that saved her husband's life have altered his thinking processes and he is currently no longer able to work, much less be left alone. One went from wife to widow, the other from wife to caregiver. They both must face their new normal.

How do we face such things? How do we walk with those who are facing these changes?

God began to talk to me about sharing on this subject. Firstly my friends, we must remember that God can handle us as well as he can handle those in our world. It takes faith. Both these women have a strong faith in Jesus, but they are also human and we must allow them to be real in their process. During the adjustment to my new normal, I knew God was good. I knew he was trustworthy, but I felt myself backing away from him at times because I was not sure what else might come my way. The amazing grace and mercy about having a relationship with Jesus is that he can handle it. He can handle our questions and pain. There is no perfect way to walk through grief and mourning. The best gift you can give someone is to be there for them, and not expect them to have to go through it in a 'certain faith way'. Remind them of God's love, grace, and mercy, and maybe even agree that it is awful, hard and you are sorry they have to go through this. You are there to walk it out with them. Don't expect them to always have the faith to walk it out on their own, let them use yours. Not with platitudes, but with the knowledge that you are praying with them and that God has His plan to help them through whatever they are facing.

Accepting the new normal takes much time. Somewhere along the process, I had to bury my old normal. I realized it was dead. The sooner I mourned and buried it, the easier it was to adjust to my new normal. I still at times long for my old married life. Comparing my old normal to the new was like comparing apples to Brussels sprouts. At the time the old (apples) would always win. Partly because I looked at my old normal through glasses of perfection. I forgot about the bruises and sour parts and only remembered the sweet things. The Holy Spirit reminded me about this one day, it was humbling. I'm actually learning to enjoy Brussels sprouts!

The comparison game is a natural part of the transition process. People would say, "What great memories you have! How wonderful." I would agree and think about how I wanted more! They are a comfort, but they are also a double-edged sword. It is much easier now to enjoy the memories but the desire for more has not really diminished.

I learned to lean and stand on Romans 8:28 NLT, *"and we know that God causes everything to work together for the good of those who love God and are called according to his purpose for them.* Decades ago, a friend was widowed and I watched God care for her. It was her story that helped hold me steady through my situation. It is my prayer that my story, even with its many variations, will help others.

My words to each of you facing your, 'new normal' are: You can do this. You can trust our God to show up with His peace and comfort. He will carry you through. Those of you who are enjoying your normal life--do it! Enjoy the blessings, love your children, take care of your health and trust your Good Good God to equip you, love you, and inspire you to help others to embrace and adjust to their new normal. We need each other. *Rejoice with those who rejoice; mourn with those who mourn, Romans 12:15 NIV.*

Father, I thank you that any shift in our 'normal' did not catch you unaware. You are always aware and are helping us walk through every change. We do not have to walk through these changes alone, for you are with us. For that, I am so grateful, even if I don't always feel it!

In Jesus' Name, amen.

11.

Faith and Loneliness

Turn to me and be gracious to me, for I am lonely and afflicted.
Psalm 25:16 NIV

Walking the widow road, I admit is often lonely and filled with potholes of opportunities to feel very isolated. Widows and widowers however are not the only lonely people in the world. It is a fact that no matter your state in life you can experience loneliness. We must all learn how to cope with loneliness. It is part of life. Debilitating loneliness often leads to discouragement and depression, which is not part of God's plan for us.

Loneliness, while difficult, can cause some very positive changes in our lives if we embrace it with faith—instead of fear or self-pity. Being alone only turns into negative loneliness when we feel isolated from God and our community. Sadness can turn into depression. Often a person feels sad and then realizes it is caused by loneliness. Once we recognize this lonely feeling, we have a choice. How do we interpret our feelings? Often our inner critical voice declares, "You are lonely because you are unlovable." This hostile judgmental advisor tries to gain control of our thoughts. If we give in to those lies, we live a much smaller life than God ever intended. I have had to fight against this voice many times. The voice likes to talk in generalities, 'everyone else' or 'no one else' and of course, we are never included in either!

The problem with loneliness is that we can begin to blame ourselves, via the critical inner voice or blame others and withdraw. You can begin to read rejection everywhere including within your marriage, family, or church. Loneliness can cause people to overspend, overeat, overdrink, become irritable, and further drive others away. We may turn to these things to try and avoid thoughts of, "poor me, I'm all alone," as they begin to increase in volume and control. These thoughts leave plenty of opportunities for the critical inner voice to magnify our negative attributes so loud that we cannot hear even the loving voices of our family, friends, or even our Savior. It is often our view of loneliness that makes a difference.

I wonder if Jesus was ever lonely. Hebrews 4:15 NLT, *This High Priest of ours understands our weaknesses, for he faced all of the same testings we do, yet he did not sin.* I think that includes loneliness. So when we feel lonely, it is good to understand that Jesus understands our loneliness. Knowing someone 'gets it' always helps me move through difficult experiences like loneliness.

So how do we break the loneliness cycle? David prayed in Psalm 25:16 NIV, *Turn to me and be gracious to me, for I am lonely and afflicted.* It can be difficult to admit to others that we are lonely, so start with the Lord. Tell him all about it, and then with eyes of faith, begin to look for ways to make the connections you need. Move toward becoming the friend you feel you need. Look for other, 'lonely people' and reach out to them. Realize that you are not the only lonely person in the world.

Understand that loneliness can be the motivation to change things in your life. It also can be a black hole that sucks you into depression and isolation. Understanding that loneliness is common to everyone is not always easy. Sometimes in some perverse way, we like to think that we and only we have it the worst. God answered David's prayer and he will answer yours as well.

One of the tools I use to fight loneliness is praise and worship. I bought myself an Amazon Dot last Christmas as a present. I don't have to put in a CD or turn on the radio. I just say, "Alexa, please play Praise and Worship." My home is instantly filled with reminders that I am not alone, and that he is with me. It really helps.

This wonderful promise found in Psalm 68 is ours. But sometimes, when we feel lonely, it is a struggle to believe it. [He is a]*Father to the fatherless, defender of widows--this is God, whose dwelling is holy. God places the lonely in families; he sets the prisoners free and gives them joy, Psalm 68:5-6 NLT.*

I will admit there have been times when I have not felt like I have found that family he talks about; but when I choose to open my eyes to those around me although I may at times be lonely, I am not alone. I use the alone times to reflect on His goodness, and the blessings I do have, and develop a thankful and grateful heart. We must realize that Satan loves to isolate and lie to God's people, and he often uses the lie of 'aloneness' and 'loneliness' to accomplish this goal. I remember one day in order to silence the critical inner voice and Satan's lies, I out loud declared, "I am part of God's family because of the work on the cross, so I am going to start acting as if I belong." It made a difference!

Father, I pray for the lonely people who struggle with feeling like part of a family. I thank you for healing the pain of loneliness in their soul and helping them connect with those around them. Bring them close to yourself and show them they are not alone.

In Jesus' Name, amen.

12.

Faith and Hitting the Wall of Discouragement

Consider him who endured from sinners such hostility against himself, so that you may not grow weary or fainthearted.
Hebrews 12:3 ESV

Discouragement comes in many forms. It feels as elusive as a nagging dread or as obvious as a dark cloud on a clear day. It can show up as heaviness or anxiety. It can feel like an oppressive wind making it hard to breathe. Discouragement comes against your feelings to try and get to your faith. We must lead by our faith, and then our feelings will come along.

The goal of the Spirit of Discouragement is to cause us to lose our motivation to accomplish valid goals. It aims to make us so emotionally fatigued and discouraged, that ultimately, we either slow down or completely stop any progress to the once purposed end. We begin to doubt if the cost is worth the effort: in short, we lose sight of the objective.

The target of discouragement is our heart and our soul: that part of us in which our emotions, will, and intellect abide. Hebrews 12:3 reminds us *to consider him who endured from sinners such hostility against himself, so that you may not grow weary or fainthearted.* We must become skilled at guarding our hearts, minds, and wills, if not, discouragement will render our courage of no effect.

Discouragement will tell you that you are weak, insecure, and unable to accomplish your God-given assignments. It seeks to derail or hinder the potency of your abilities. It seeks to undermine every area of your life. Occupations, marriage, parenting and even basic relationships can fall victim to its subtleties, but thanks be to God, we have a Savior who stands with us against this threat. Do not put up with Satan's tactics in these areas. God's word is strong and powerful against the wiles of the enemy. The walls of discouragement are not so thick that they cannot be broken through.

In the gospels, we find the disciples in hiding after they heard the most discouraging news possible. Their leader Jesus, had been arrested, crucified, and buried. They ran back to their homes, huddling in fear and discouragement. Maybe they wondered if they had wasted three years of their lives. Then, the women came with amazing news! Jesus was alive! They heard the truth, not the facts. As we stand on God's truth, the 'facts' that Satan tries to throw in our faces are rendered powerless. What may look like death in your life, with God's help, can be the beginning of life. Friends, remember as we walk with our Savior he is working all things together for his good, which means our good as well. This is our hope.

We fight discouragement by turning our eyes away from the discouraging things facing us and putting our eyes on our God. We begin to take courage from him. In 1 Thessalonians 2:2 NLT, Paul writes, "*You know how badly we had been treated at Philippi just before we came to you and how much we suffered there. Yet our God gave us the courage to declare his Good News to you boldly, despite great opposition.*

When you begin to notice this evil force assailing you:

1. Take a break from what you are doing.
2. Look at Jesus and turn to his Word, the Truth!
3. Take the authority given you by the Scriptures.
4. Begin to meditate on him and what he has done for you.
5. Remind yourself of answered prayers and testimonies from yourself and others.
6. Ask the Holy Spirit for help.
7. Do not isolate yourself but develop strong relationships; we gain encouragement and courage from our brothers and sisters.
8. Take time to sing and worship him.
9. Declare your intentions with his help to break through this wall of discouragement.

I am no longer surprised when I come face to face with the wall of discouragement. I have learned to recognize its subtleties, hopefully, sooner than later. When I am tired, hungry, or feel alone, discouragement tries to come calling at my door. I have learned not to let it in—even if at times, I admit we might have discussions at the door! Press through dear friend, and keep your eyes on the Lord and his plans for your life. It is worth it. Bring those thoughts captive and thank him for your freedom from discouragement.

Therefore do not cast away your confidence, which has great reward. For you have need of endurance, so that after you have done the will of God, you may receive the promise: For yet a little while, And He who is coming will come and will not tarry. Now the just shall live by faith; But if anyone draws back, my soul has no pleasure in him. Hebrews 10:35-38 NKJV

Father, I thank you for giving us the strength to overcome the walls of discouragement that come our way. I thank you that we can lean on your strength and purpose when we feel weak. Help us to choose to walk by faith—not fear or doubt.

In Jesus' Name, amen.

13.

Faith and God's Yes's and No's

Paul and his companions traveled throughout the region of Phrygia and Galatia, having been kept by the Holy Spirit from preaching the word in the province of Asia. Acts 16:6 NIV

Acts 16 tells the story of some of the Apostle Paul's travels. He and his friends felt it was time to go and share the gospel with more people. It was the second of his missionary journeys and I am sure he was eager to see what God was going to do. Sometimes we forget that Paul was a human like us. He had to learn to follow God's leading, just like we do. We are fortunate that he wrote his stories so we can learn from them.

Paul and Silas had a plan in obedience to Christ's instructions, they would take the gospel, to *go and make disciples of all nations...," Matthew 28:19 NIV.* I assume Paul and Silas knew of these instructions. So how do you think they felt when they passed through Phrygia and Galatia and the Holy Spirit forbid them to proclaim the Word in Asia as described in Acts 16:6? Then they tried to go into Bithynia and again they weren't permitted to go. If it were me, I probably would have either been frustrated or excited! If these were the no's, what will God's yeses be? *So they passed by Mysia and went down to Troas. During the night Paul had a vision of a man of Macedonia standing and begging him, "Come over to Macedonia and help us." After Paul had seen the vision, we got ready at once to leave for Macedonia, concluding that God had called us to preach the gospel to them. Acts 16:8-10*

Finally, a God yes! When we are waiting for our yes, especially after many no's, there can be the temptation to believe there are no yeses. We can feel we are going to be stuck where we are forever and that God must have forgotten about us. Waiting on him becomes a time of testing our resolve, our trust, and definitely our patience.

I remember when we felt God's call to leave Oregon and move to Washington, one of the major steps we needed to do was sell our home of nine years. We got it ready, put it on the market, and then waited.

And waited.

And waited.

We encouraged ourselves in the Lord and we waited.

"Ok Lord, we only need one buyer, just one!"

We waited some more.

No nibbles, not many showings.

We kept waiting.

The summer was drawing to a close and school was due to begin in Washington for our children. What do we do? We decided to go ahead and make the move, even without the sale. We rented a truck and began packing it. We stopped keeping our house in 'show mode' and just went to packing. One Saturday a realtor stopped by unannounced, asking if he could show it to his clients. Darryl said, OK. I was out on an errand and was not home at the time.

Darryl felt the Holy Spirit say, "These people are going to buy your home."

They left without a word. A few hours later, their realtor called and said they wanted to make an offer. It was a low ball offer, but because of us packing and moving when they arrived, they felt they could get a 'real' deal. Darryl felt the Holy Spirit say to turn down the deal. So we said no.

"NO." What?

While we were eating our last supper in the house before our big move, sitting on the floor in the kitchen, the phone rang. Our counter-offer was accepted! The house was sold! We left for Washington with much freer hearts. We waited and waited for a buyer all those months and then at our, 'last minute' one came. In God's time, his 'no and wait' turned to 'yes'.

During waiting times, we can get frustrated with others and distracted from our call. Comparison with others' stories can make us feel unloved or uncared for by the Lord or, we can choose to develop patient trust and thankfulness for what he has already done. During your waiting season, look to your testimonies or the testimonies of others. Let's rehearse his goodness. Let your stories remind you of his faithfulness and like Peter, declare that you *have the words of eternal life, John 6:68 NKJV*. Peter, chose to trust Jesus. He had been with him and knew His character and His faithfulness. If we want to walk in God's ways then by necessity, we will eventually have to go back to trusting him anyways!

It is not easy having faith during waiting times. Listening to the no's and wondering where the yeses are can lead to discouragement. We must remember he has them in His timings and His ways. Whether you too are in a time of waiting for a house to sell, a marriage partner, a new job, or other direction, you can trust His no's as well as His yes's, for he is a trustworthy God.

Father, I thank you for helping us trust you when things are delayed. I thank you for reminding us of your faithfulness in our lives, and how you have answered prayers for others that God will answer our prayers as well. I am sure Paul and Silas were perplexed with your no's, but it didn't stop them from moving on. Help us to do the same.

In Jesus' Name, amen.

14.

Faith and God's Good Grace

...My grace is all you need. My power works best in weakness.
2 Corinthians 12:9 NLT

Wow, I am still struggling to understand and embrace my weaknesses. It takes courage to look at them. It takes courage and humility to admit the weaknesses are there. Paul writes in 2 Corinthians 12:8-9, *"Three times I pleaded with the Lord to relieve me of this. But he answered me, "My grace is always more than enough for you, and my power finds its full expression through your weakness."* Even though we don't clearly know or understand Paul's thorn or weakness, we know he did, and so did the Lord. He took the time to ask the Lord three times for it to be removed, and he finally came to a place of peace concerning it. The Passion Translation goes on to say, *"So I will celebrate my weaknesses, for when I'm weak I sense more deeply the mighty power of Christ living in me."* Learning to lean on the Lord and acknowledging our weakness allows us to rely on the power of the Holy Spirit, not our power and ability.

Every weakness is an opportunity to release this power to work in and through us.

This past week has been busy. I started teaching astronomy and health to four of my grandchildren, plus our Life Group began a new study with new people! My son and his wife took a Covid-delayed 10th-anniversary getaway, so I helped with their children as well. Other projects popped up and let's just say it's been a full week. My 'thorn' during this season seems to be tiredness. The things on my to-do list were not budging. My solution was to begin the day talking to the Lord about it and thanking him for the strength I needed to not only do the tasks but to do it cheerfully and with strength. I was able to accomplish even more than I felt I could do.

In verse 10 Paul says, *So I'm not defeated by my weakness, but delighted! 2 Corinthians 12:10 TPT.* I admit after I acknowledged my need for him, I was blessed and excited about how I had the energy I needed to love on my grandchildren as they needed.

When was the last time you felt delighted by your weakness? I admit I came home and rested, but the patience, grace, and focus I needed were there when I needed them. Paul continues: *For when I feel my weakness and endure mistreatment—when I'm surrounded with troubles on every side and face persecution because of my love* for Christ—I am made yet stronger. For my weakness becomes a portal to God's power.

I know *my* weakness is so small compared to all the troubles and trials Paul faced, but when I stopped being frustrated by it, admitted it, and then asked for help, I could complete my godly assignment. What I love about God's grace is that it is sufficient for both the big and the small things of life.

It doesn't matter what it is. His grace is accessible for all things. All we have to do is position ourselves to receive it. This positioning includes the admission of our weakness to him. In other words, we must humble ourselves. Then we can release our faith, so that when we ask, we will receive. So then, we allow that gracious provision to show up as he deems. It may be through help from others or the courage to tackle the job ourselves, but it will show up in a way that will show forth his power and grace; giving him the glory, and isn't that what we want to do with our lives?

Maybe you need his grace to overcome resentment, bitterness, or other works of the flesh, as described in Galatians 5:19-21. His grace is available to you. Perhaps you struggle with addictions or feelings of unworthiness. His grace is available to you. Ephesians 2:8 NKJV declares, *"For by grace you have been saved through faith, and that not of yourselves; it is* the gift of God.*"*

We began our journey by faith because of the grace of God, and it is the only way we can continue. Do not shortchange the grace of God and your need for it in your life. It is the only way to live, relying on him and his ways. If you stumble, rely on his grace to forgive, and then get back up. Rely on his grace to keep you walking straight. It is incredible, this gift of grace we have been given—don't let it go to waste in your life. Access it every day in every way. Your life will improve!

Father, I thank you for your amazing grace. It's so abundant. You never run out of it. Help us to rely on you and your strength every day. You love it when we do. It brings you glory and joy. Teach us to rely on you even more.

In Jesus' Name, amen.

15.

Faith and Groanings

For in this tent, we groan, longing to put on our heavenly dwelling.
2 Corinthians 5:2 ESV

There it goes again, another bit of sad difficult news that already is adding to my soul burden. I find myself letting out a big sigh and maybe even a groan or two as I process the information. How about you? A family member with relationship issues, a bad diagnosis from the doctor, the struggle of discernment between truth and distortion in the news—all can lead to a sense of overwhelming burden and care.

Reading Romans 8:26-27 NLT, this morning was so comforting and reassuring. *And the Holy Spirit helps us in our weakness. For example, we don't know what God wants us to pray for. But the Holy Spirit prays for us with groanings that cannot be expressed in words. And the Father who knows all hearts knows what the Spirit is saying, for the Spirit pleads for us believers in harmony with God's own will.* To remind us of how we have the Holy Spirit who not only understands our groans and sighs but comes alongside us to help us in those moments.

Groan: a low, mournful sound uttered in pain or grief. Science tells us that the act of groaning is a primal way of releasing stress. It stimulates the part of your brain that helps assess whether you are safe or not. When people are in intense physical pain they often moan and groan—scientific studies have shown people tolerate pain longer if they can moan. Interestingly, several scriptures refer to the groaning and moaning that women make in labor—often a coping mechanism to work through the intensity of childbirth, which means that sometimes we groan and moan while we are producing good fruit!

Sigh: to let out one's breath audibly, as from sorrow, weariness, or relief. Sighing also has a physical benefit. Many times when we hear difficult news we unconsciously hold our breath. Sighing is the way our body gets rid of any excess CO_2 and the deep breath after helps us take in more oxygen.

The good news is Isaiah 51:11 ESV tells us that there will come a day when *the ransomed of the LORD shall return and come to Zion with singing; everlasting joy shall be upon their heads; they shall obtain gladness and joy, and sorrow and sighing shall flee away.*

I think in our present season of Covid and violence, I find myself groaning and sighing much more often. I have heard many people, believers and unbelievers alike, responding to difficult news with, "Oh God!" Even people who don't normally give him a thought seem to without a thought, call on his name! The help he gives us, does not replace our prayers, but he helps us to pray them. I believe that he initially reminds us that our God is present! He wants to help us turn to him. To help us look up and out from those circumstances that would seek to crush us.

When I begin to move from the moans and groans to actual words in prayer, I find the Holy Spirit leading me from honest overwhelming moans and sighs to words of hope and solution-finding. It is almost like he maps out a journey as I keep praying and he leads me from the wilderness towards the promised land. Often my cloudy thinking begins to clear and I can begin to see where to take the next step. I know it is him helping me navigate the dark difficult waters of confusion and even at times, despair.

I want to encourage you not to ignore your groanings. Not to pretend they aren't there, but to acknowledge them to the Lord and actively bring him into those dark areas. Our national political situation often causes me to want to hide under the covers! It is the Word of God and the Holy Spirit that lead me to pray for our leaders and nation; asking the God of all Nations to bring his solutions to play. To protect the truth and to even show us how to vote! There are so many opinions flying around and I find myself simply asking the Lord to uncover the truth and lead me to it! The Holy Spirit helps encourage me to stand strong and face every groaning and moaning I experience, and he desires to do the same for each of us.

Father, I ask that you alert us to our moanings, groanings, and sighings. I ask that as we acknowledge the stressful season we live in that you teach us how to access your help even more. We release our faith for not only solutions to our personal needs, but also for the global situations our world is facing. We pray that you will uncover the truth wherever it has been hidden, twisted, or manipulated in any area of our lives. We thank you for helping us to continue to stand strong as believers and not shy away from things that would produce more sighing and groaning, but that we would trust you in the midst of them.

In Jesus' Name, amen.

16.

Faith and Help

I sought the Lord, and he answered me and delivered me
from all my fears. Psalm 34:4 ESV

I have been joining with many women of our church in a Bible study called Amen. It is subtitled, 'the story of Scripture from Eden to Eternity'. The goal is to gain a deeper comprehension of God's purpose and plan for history as it's presented in the entire Bible. As we journey through this overview of the greatest story on earth, I am reminded once again how humanity needed a Savior. Reading about the shortcomings of Saul, David, and Solomon reminds me of my own. I am so grateful we have a Savior. His name is Jesus, and we can know him intimately.

If you struggle today, please remind yourself that you too have a Savior. Look to him. Do not do life on your own. No matter what the struggle, he is there. Ready to help, ready to walk through any storm, difficulty, and situation.

I want to remind you, he is a perfect gentleman. He does not come in unless we ask him to. Yes, he is a good Father who watches over our lives but to receive the most of his care we must ask, seek and pursue him and his ways. We must be honest with ourselves and with him. This is not always easy because we don't always want to admit our needs.

Lessons I've learned in receiving help from the Savior:

1. Go to him sooner than later. Don't wait until you are feeling over-whelmed but learn to go to him with the smaller issues before they become large.
2. Don't let your past delays stop you from going to him if your issues are now large!
3. Admit you need his help.
4. Repent if you need to, receive his forgiveness and forgive yourself.
5. Remind yourself of Bible stories where he helped others, or of your own past help stories.
6. Obey his advice, even if it means humbling yourself.
7. Trust his direction.
8. Be patient to wait for his answers.
9. Keep on walking in his ways, let his peace guard your heart.

I sought the Lord, and he answered me and delivered me from all my fears. Psalm 34:4 ESV

The righteous cry out, and the Lord hears, And delivers them out of all their troubles. Psalm 34:17 NKJV

When anxiety was great within me, your consolation brought me joy. Psalm 94:19 NIV

For I am convinced that neither death nor life, neither angels nor demons, neither the present nor the future, nor any powers, neither height nor depth, nor anything else in all creation, will be able to separate us from the love of God that is in Christ Jesus our Lord. Romans 8:38-39 NIV

Trust in the Lord with all your heart and lean not on your own under-standing; in all your ways submit to him, and he will make your paths straight. Proverbs 3:5-6 NIV

Do not be anxious about anything, but in every situation, by prayer and petition, with thanksgiving, present your requests to God. And the peace of God, which transcends all understanding, will guard your hearts and minds in Christ Jesus. Philippians 4:6-7 NIV

Father, I am so grateful you are with us. I am grateful for your help. All I have to do is call upon your Name and you are there. Remind me when I forget, ok?

In Jesus' Name, amen.

17.

Faith and Preparing for Life's Storms

Anyone who listens to my teaching and follows it is wise,
like a person who builds a house on solid rock. Though the rain
comes in torrents and the floodwaters rise and the winds beat
against that house, it won't collapse because it is built on bedrock.
Matthew 7:24-25 NLT

How prepared are we for life's storms? Some are expected, and many are not. My local climate zone is called temperate. This means we don't see many life-threatening storms, but each winter we may lose power once or twice for a few hours. A few years ago, however, my home was without power for three days. I live on an island and the major power connection was disrupted by downed trees. We were fortunate. We had wood for our wood stove, batteries for our flashlights, and food that we could prepare on top of our woodstove.

We were able to take in a family, who having just moved from sunny California did not even own winter coats! They lived in an apartment that had none of those luxuries—warmth or a way to cook. We were just getting acquainted with them and they had asked to meet with Darryl and me that very morning. By God's grace and faithfulness, we were able to take this family of four into our home because of our preparedness.

Even as we were prepared for physical storms, the Lord encourages us to make sure our foundations are built on the solid rock of Jesus Christ and his word. Rain falls on the just and the unjust the scripture says. Life's storms can be overwhelming and challenging. Yet, we can be prepared. Just as we prepare for potential power outages as weather alerts or warnings appear, so we can prepare for the storms of life.

First, check your gear. Take an assessment of where you are now. What areas do you feel solid in your faith? What areas do you find yourself struggling in? Do not be afraid of your weak areas. It is much better to find out you are missing batteries for your flashlight before the storm hits than to discover it after the power goes out. Concentrate on building up these weak areas with the promises in his word.

One summer, I had to face the fact that some areas of my roof and siding were rotten. I was afraid it was going to cost a lot emotionally, financially, and physically. As I gained the courage to ask people who knew how to assess the problem, I discovered it was much easier to repair than my imagination led me to believe. The fear of the task was much bigger than just getting it done! Ask the Lord to show you your weak areas. He will do so in love and grace, and also bring the solution!

Once that assessment has been made, it is time to gather what you need. Take the time to explore what God's word has to say to strengthen those weaker areas. Commit to not only reading it but applying it. Remember, the information does not transform us; it is the application of that knowledge that begins the transforming work. I find that I may need to slow down my reading of God's word and allow the Holy Spirit to really talk to me about what I am reading to make it clear.

Find your encouraging team. Get connected to a community of believers. Not just attend a church, but choose to get involved. Not just doing tasks together, but developing friendships through small group connections is so life-giving. Ask God to open your eyes to those who need your friendship and reach out to them. I love my Life Group. They are amazing ladies who care for each other. Doing life together through all seasons helps weave a blanket of warmth and care. We are learning to share our needs, as well as our strengths. One of the interesting side-effects of enduring a storm together is that it creates history. Enduring storms and overcoming them together builds depth and kinship in your relationships. Praying for one another during challenges helps us celebrate together when they are over.

Seek out those who have gone through storms and trials gracefully. Ask for their wisdom. Talk to the 'old timers', and ask them to share their wisdom and experience. A wise person learns from those who have gone before. Let them be honest! Be willing to share your stories as well. When my husband passed, I read the stories of others who walked my same path. The hope I began to glean from their struggles and victories was like a lifeline to me. Pride often keeps us isolated during storms. A man named Harry R. Truman refused to leave his home despite evacuation orders due to the impending volcanic eruption of Mt. St. Helens in 1980. He lost his life because he did not heed the warning. His stubbornness cost him his life.

In stormy seasons, decide to come alongside those who are in the midst of challenges you might not have faced yourself. Check on your neighbors. Support them the best you can. Ask them how you can help. Be available. It will help prepare you for your storms as well.

Seek wisdom: Plan on getting married? Prepare by reading books, and talking with others who have a good marriage. Becoming a parent? Join a MOPS group, and read blogs and books from trusted wise parents who have run the race ahead of you. Financial issues? Seek help. Can't seem to get along with others? Get some counseling or tools to learn how to communicate. We all have emotions. We all need to learn how to handle them so they don't handle us! Get prepared!

Help prepare others. One day at a Mother-Daughter Tea with my mom, I realized that her job was to prepare me to live without her. I began my own child-rearing season with the understanding I needed to prepare my children for life and its challenges. I'm not sure if I got it all right, but at least I tried. I continue to do the same through loving, caring, and teaching my grandchildren.

Challenges come in many forms. By applying God's words, we have the luxury of joining with the Boy Scouts and their motto: BE PREPARED through every type of storm—both natural and metaphorical. Let's choose to see the storms of life as adventurous adventures where we can watch our God show up with His power, might, and grace.

Father, I ask that you reveal our strengths and weaknesses in you. Show us how to build on that solid rock, that we can trust. I thank you that you do not leave us alone to face the storms of life, but you are very present with us. We trust you to help us build on the solid rock of your ways and your will.

In Jesus' Name, amen

18.

Faith and the Battle

During those dark times, it was not safe to travel.
Problems troubled the people of every land.
2 Chronicles 15:5 NLT

Sometimes we journey through seasons of "dark times". They may occur after a season of victories, or they may show up during a time when you see little or no progress. In the United States, like in other countries, we are faced with some serious issues that have led to death and destruction. A few weeks ago a young woman was killed protesting other protestors in Charlottesville. Many were killed in Spain around the same time, the murder weapon a car in both situations.

As I was reading my devotions, I came across 2 Chronicles 15:5. I was amazed at how accurate it described our present-day scenario, *"During those dark times, it was not safe to travel. Problems troubled the people of every land. Nation fought against nation, and city against city, for God was troubling them with every kind of problem."* Wow! I am not so bold as to say **God** is troubling us. I do know that he can use and is using these problems our sinful natures have created, to promote his purpose and plans.

I know these kinds of reports affect my spirit. I admit I do have to fight what I call 'turtling up'. Drawing my head and heart inside and hiding away through distractions, busyness, or depression. I am so thankful for the next verse. It gives us clear instruction, *"But as for you, be strong and courageous, for your work will be rewarded," 2 Chronicles 15:7NLT.*

The chronicler is speaking clearly to you and me, be STRONG! Be COURAGEOUS! This is not the time to drawback, but it is a time to press in, using all the weaponry at our disposal. Ephesians 6:10-12 NLT says, "... *Be strong in the Lord and in his mighty power. Put on all of God's armor so that you will be able to stand firm against all strategies of the devil. For we are not fighting against flesh-and-blood enemies, but against evil rulers and authorities of the unseen world, against mighty powers in this dark world, and against evil spirits in the heavenly places."*

God has called and positioned each of us in our sphere of influence to bring light into this world. We can do everything he has called us to do. My Police Chaplain friend Bill Hinckley, was asked first by the Lord and then his friend Mark to go with him to Virginia. Unfortunately, that young woman killed in Charlottesville was Mark's daughter. Bill called asking for prayer as they made the journey. God went before them. They discovered grace, peace, and supportive care as they traveled. They also encountered the Spirit of Division and hate that was the source of the rallies that took Heather's life. Bill shared with me that as he prayed, he watched attitudes change and love prevail. We must remember we are in a spiritual battle. The main war, of course, was completed on the cross by Jesus; however, we must fight to bring the freedom he died for into our lives. It may seem easier to just surrender to the blahs, depression, or discouragement, but at what cost? Our enemy will continue to try to take more and more from us.

Therefore, put on every piece of God's armor so you will be able to resist the enemy in the time of evil. Then after the battle you will still be standing firm. Ephesians 6:13 (NLT) God desires that we come through these battles with victory. My family seems to be having their share of battles lately, but we are all determined to come through still standing; not only for ourselves but also for the next generation. It is definitely not all about us. *So, my dear brothers and sisters, be strong and immovable. Always work enthusiastically for the Lord, for you know that nothing you do for the Lord is ever useless.* 1 Corinthians 15:58 (NLT).

Father, I thank you for reminding us of the gift of the Armor you've given us. Teach us to use each part. I thank you for strengthening us in the midst of our battles, causing us to stand firm and not give way to the enemy. When the fight seems overwhelming, remind us that we are called to work enthusiastically for you, and it is not a waste.

In Jesus' Name, amen.

19.

Faith and the Middle

When you pass through the waters, I will be with you;
and through the rivers, they shall not overwhelm you;
when you walk through the fire you shall not be burned,
and the flame shall not consume you. Isaiah 43:2 (ESV)

A normal pregnancy ends with the birthing process. I have been pregnant three times. The way my body is made, for some reason I never experienced the urge to push. Consequently, when I grew weary from the pain of back labor with my son, I just stopped pushing. I quit. I lay back on the bed and stopped any active part on my behalf to get that baby born. My doctor looked at Darryl and said, "She has to do this." Darryl looked at me and said, "Come on honey, you can do this." The nurse leaned over and whispered, "Come on, you can do this. Soon you will be holding your little baby in your arms and we will all leave you alone!"

The doctor's words, even Darryl's words were not motivation enough for me to resume action; it was the kind nurse who seemed to understand my need that got me back in the game.

We do get tired in the middle. Especially if we don't know how long the race is or where the finish line is! I had been pushing for a while, but could not gauge exactly where I was in the process. I was tired. I had been de-lousing my daughters' hair all day and then went into labor. I was exhausted. Sometimes life is messy and storms, struggles, and warfare show up when we already feel weak. I was reading the book of Judges last week and came across a story that is not fun to read, but the application is so encouraging that I want to share it.

You can read the story in Judges 20. Due to some unfortunate choices and incidents, all the Israelites were united in a fight against their brother tribe Benjamin. The back story begins in Judges 19, but in 20 we find them seeking the Lord for his will and purpose. They first tried negotiations, but the Benjamites refused to give up the men responsible for the uproar. They chose to fight their brethren.

Before the battle, the Israelites went to Bethel and asked God, "Which tribe should go first to attack the people of Benjamin?" The Lord answered, "Judah is to go first." So the Israelites left early the next morning and camped near Gibeah. Then they advanced toward Gibeah to attack the men of Benjamin. m*But Benjamin's warriors, who were defending the town, came out and killed 22,000 Israelites on the battlefield that day. Judges 20:18-21 (NLT)*

Wow. What a defeat. They assumed they would win because their cause was just and they had heard God's strategy, "Send Judah first," but they lost. Did they give up? No. They went back to the Lord.

But the Israelites encouraged each other and took their positions again at the same place they had fought the previous day. For they had gone up to Bethel and wept in the presence of the Lord until evening. They had asked the *Lord, "Should we fight against our relatives from Benjamin again?" And the Lord* had said, "Go out and fight against them." *So the* next day they went out again to fight against the men of Benjamin, but the men of Benjamin killed another 18,000 Israelites, all of whom were experienced with the sword. Then all the Israelites went up to Bethel and wept in the presence of the Lord and fasted until evening. They also brought burnt offerings and peace offerings to the Lord. The Israelites went up seeking direction from the Lord. (In those days the Ark of the Covenant of God was in Bethel, and Phinehas son of Eleazar and grandson of Aaron was the priest.) The Israelites asked the Lord, "Should we fight against our relatives from Benjamin again, or should we stop?" The Lord said, "Go! Tomorrow I will hand them over to you." Judges 20:22-28 (NLT)

Three times they sought the Lord. Even though they were defeated twice, they did not give up. They continued seeking him and his ways. We too, must not give up in the middle of the battle. We must move on. Before we begin, we must count the cost to our best ability according to Luke 14:28; then we must determine to move forward. If we quit in the middle, we will only feel shame, guilt, and defeat. Don't quit fighting the battle for your marriage, your children, or your loved ones.

Keep on until there is clarity from the Lord and a release from the battle. We may lose some battles, but we know God has already won the war. So press on. Encourage yourself with worship, the word, and fellowship with others, but press on. Do not quit. Take a break if you need to, but do so with the end in sight.

Keep on, my dear friend. We do not fight against flesh and blood, but against principalities in high places, so make sure you are not fighting a spiritual battle with fleshly tools. Stay prayed up, full of the word, and always remember, greater is he that is in you than he that is in the world.

Father, I thank you for helping us to keep fighting—even in the middle of the storm. I thank you for your courage to help us pass through the fire, through the waters, and onto peaceful shores. Help me to turn *to you in my discouragement and weariness. Help me to walk in peace during these times, knowing that I am not alone and that you are with me. Thank you.*

In Jesus' Name, amen

20.

Faith and Vulnerable Times

Put on the full armor of God,
so that you can take your stand against the devil's schemes.
Ephesians 6:11(NIV)

I don't know about you, but I am very well aware of how the battle rages. So many friends, family members, and even ministries are going through some difficult seasons right now. My heart hurts for those who have unexpectedly lost loved ones, those who are battling severe sicknesses or struggles with their children, marriages, or finances. It's hard.

I am going, to be honest here. I know there are spiritual battles trying to get us to quit believing in a God that is powerful and who answers prayer. These battles want us to think it doesn't matter whether or not we live holy and righteously.

Sometimes, I just want to ignore these battles. To put my head in the sand and think if I just leave it there long enough, the problem will go away. Not true. Every time I try to choose that option, I realize nothing changes unless it's deterioration. I am vulnerable in my choice to fight. Will my weariness or my personal struggles cause me to choose the ostrich option? Or do I stand tall in the whole armor of the Lord, girding my loins with his truth?

This past Sunday morning, after having a miserable night's sleep, I was tempted to stay in bed and watch the service online; justifying to myself that I deserved the rest as my body just did not want to get up and do my usual Sunday morning routine. To top it off, the older friend I usually bring to church was not coming that day. It was almost too easy to convince myself that nobody would know or care if I stayed home. This was a very small battle, but I decided to bring my body subject and get up and get ready. It was a choice I am glad I made.

Another time of vulnerability is when we feel we are alone. Maybe we don't sense anyone else has entered the battle. We stand at the place of choice and look for someone else to join, but maybe the Lord is asking us to take the first stand. Others may be standing along the sidelines waiting for a leader to step up, and you are that leader. Capturing fears of inadequacy, weariness, apathy, or discouragement is crucial to moving forward in the battle.

Sometimes when we fight, there is a loss. In my optimistic worldview, I want to believe every battle is a win, but in truth, though the war is won, we can suffer setbacks in battles. The promise that everything will work together for good, is so encouraging during these seasons. Stubborn illnesses that seem resistant to the name of Jesus, prodigal children walking away for years, and spouses who abandon marriages can all feel like defeat.

Fighting the 'why bother' thoughts is often a very real struggle; another point of vulnerability. Take heart. This very week I heard of two long-term adult prodigals who have returned to the flock! Their parents endured years of struggle as they watched their offspring being derailed by addictions and poor choices. They fought feelings of shame, discouragement, and hopelessness and persevered. Keep on believing my friend. Stand in the gap. Please know your Heavenly Father has wayward children also. He understands.

Points of vulnerability occur when we feel we have too many battlefronts. We get overwhelmed and want to quit. God says, stand and see the salvation of your God. We may need to retreat and re-group. Reading through the Apostle Paul's battles and struggles encourages me to stand. Taking time to make our God big again through worship, the word, and fellowship can make the difference between quitting and moving ahead. Listen to the Holy Spirit. He may lead you aside to rest. Take time to nourish your body. Take a walk. Enjoy his creation. Replenish your soul. These are important battle tools as well. Remember Elijah? Take time to read his story in 1 Kings 19.

The other day my Microsoft computer, shouted at me, "Stop! You are vulnerable," among other things. I was so shocked I didn't know what to do. I called my son and had him listen. I asked him what to do and he advised me to shut it off so I did. I am writing this on my Kindle Fire. I took a bit of a break and my saved draft disappeared. I have retyped it by finding my saved draft on my iPhone. I am pushing forward because I feel I need to publish this today. Somebody needs this.

Stand strong my friends. We are victorious in him.

Father, I ask you to reveal any points of vulnerability we have. I thank you for helping us strengthen those weak areas. Make us sensitive to the enemy and his ways. We choose to stand strong, wearing your armor, loud and proud. Remind us that in you, we have the power to overcome.

In Jesus' Name, amen.

21.

Faith and Dealing with Anxiety

Casting all your care upon Him, for He cares for you.
I Peter 5:7 (NKJV)

I think most people in this day and age would agree that these are stressful times. Maybe more stressful on our soul, body, and spirits than usual. This week I've encountered sad news, bad news, and distressing encounters. How about you? I've also had some good news, happy news, and answers to prayer! The Lord showed me that the negative news seems to cling much longer than the positive.

The first thing we have to do is accept the fact that these kinds of things do touch our souls. None of us are impervious to the effects of difficulties. As much as I like to think the perfect me can carry and deal with hard things, I have to admit I can't, but he can.

So what does that mean? It takes time and deliberate steps to process the negative news and give it over to the Lord. *Give all your worries and cares to God, for He cares about you. I Peter 5: 7 NLT* The King James version uses the word *cast.* Either way, there must be a transfer from us to him. Anxiety and cares in the Greek translation is *mermna.* From *meiro 'to divide' and noos, 'the mind'.* Anxieties and cares come into our lives to divide our thoughts and distract us from his thoughts and his ways. *Merimna* means to be anxious beforehand about daily life. We have a Savior who is looking after those things. It is not our portion. When things come fast and furious at us, it is hard to take the time to do the transfer, but we must do so. An often missing step is to pray about the situation, but not do the transfer. I have had to slow down and prayerfully, give him every care.

As I focus on him, his ways and his words, my faith, and trust grow so I can truly make the transfer. Then it is up to him how he chooses to answer these prayers.

Search me O God, and know my heart; test me and know my anxious thoughts. Point out anything in me that offends you, and lead me along the path of everlasting life. Psalm 139:23-24 (NLT)

Understand that he already knows every area of our thought life. I encourage you to read the entire Psalm. It is so encouraging and uplifting. God knows those areas of our hearts that trouble us. Do not fear praying this prayer. It is often the first step to greater freedom in our walk with him. He searches with grace and mercy, but also with truth, and that truth always brings freedom. Freedom from guilt, shame, and the resulting anxiety from carrying such emotions us with. When we take time to pray these 'transfer' prayers, the Holy Spirit often points out areas where we need to grow in trust, or allow his finished work on the cross to be applied. Revelation 12:11 tells us that we overcome by the blood of the Lamb and by the word of their testimony.

This week as I received the sad news, bad news, and even disturbing news I made a conscious effort to focus on the positive news. At our Life

Group, I listened with intent to the God stories the ladies shared. I asked them to pray for some of my requests and their caring prayers touched my heart. We need the two or three believing in agreement oftentimes to help us know we are not alone.

As I took the time to transfer my cares to him, joy came. Peace came. Hope came. It took time, but I was with him and that was good! I encourage you to do the same. Make it a habit!

Father, I thank you that you care, not only for me but for those things I care about. I ask you to show us how to walk in your peace, not in anxiety. Show us how to capture those anxious thoughts before they affect our actions.

In Jesus' Name, amen.

22.

Faith and Struggling with Weaknesses

But he said to me, "My grace is sufficient for you, for my power is made perfect in weakness." Therefore I will boast all the more gladly of my weaknesses, so that the power of Christ may rest upon me. *Corinthians 12:9 (ESV)*

Have you ever seen a video where a person or animal is stuck in water, mud, or quicksand? Rescuers come to help, and the person is so scared they fight against their own rescuers? I think many of us are reluctant to admit to soul weakness or spiritual weakness. The Lord sends someone with advice and we choose to continue to struggle by ourselves and with ourselves! It seems to be against our fleshly nature to want to admit any weakness, so it seems to me.

What I've learned is when we find ourselves feeling weak, we must first humble ourselves and admit it. Difficult for our prideful souls, is it? Once we admit our lack, we can appeal to the Lord and to others for help.

It may be health struggles, emotional issues, or a lack of confidence in our ability to make the right choices. These are all areas where we can lean on him.

So many times believers try to muster up the strength they need to overcome their weak areas, instead of inviting the Holy Spirit to come to where they are and lead them out of their struggles. One of my 'weaker areas' has been walking through grief. I admit I've tried a lot of different tactics to deal with the pain of loss. I have tried to ignore it. I have tried to shame my way out of it by telling myself, "It's been so long, shame on you for dealing with this again." I've tried to suck it up and put on a cheerful face but, it is not until I sit down with the Lord and ask him to walk with me in it, that I find the rest and strength I need. I've learned to make friends with grief. I received his power as I admit my need.

My body has a weakness. Years ago, I made a mistake and mixed ammonia and bleach together to make a DIY cleaning product. I learned the hard way after I damaged my lungs, breathing in the fumes. So now I deal with asthma. It's humbling and embarrassing but until healing is manifested, the Lord and I walk together with it. I call on him frequently for his help, and he is always there.

It is freeing to know that he is with me, both in grief and asthma! Surrendering your expectations of living a perfect life is so freeing. That is why we needed a Savior in the first place. Please my friends, do not do life with your own strength! He is there waiting to help you and me. Paul also wrestled with weakness. He told the church in Corinth about God's response when he wanted to be freed from his weakness. *But he said to me, "My grace is sufficient for you, for my power is made perfect in weakness."* Therefore I will boast all the more gladly of my weaknesses, so that the power of Christ may rest upon me. *2 Corinthians 12:9* (ESV)

When we admit our weaknesses, the same ones our God already knows we have; our God stories will increase. His name will be lifted up as we rely on his strength, wisdom, and power more and more. Let us boldly bring them to our Loving Father.

Father, I thank you for helping us come to terms with our weaknesses. Please help us not let our pride come in between us, that we will lean on your grace. We ask that your power be made evident in our situations and circumstances as we learn to lean.

In Jesus' Name, amen.

23.

Faith and "Dealing with Disappointment"

Being confident of this very thing, that He who began a good work
in you will carry it to completion until the day of Christ Jesus.
Philippians 1:6 (NIV)

Tomorrow I am supposed to jump in my car and drive five plus hours to meet up with two old friends with their friends for a prayer retreat. When I say old friends, these two special ladies knew me before I got married! In fact, they were at our wedding. 48 years ago! What an out of the blue, off the radar invitation. But, I have been fighting a virus this week. The coughing, congested feel like you've been drained of every energy type of virus. So here I sit, resting, praying and dealing with the possible disappointment that I won't have the energy or health to make the trip.

I thought about the phrase "dealing with disappointment". I pictured someone taking the different "cards" of my situation and spreading them out on a table. First is my emotions card. What is the source of my disappointment? First, there are no do-overs. This is a onetime shot. One friend, Kay, lives in Arizona, the other, Malana, in Alaska! Apparently, they have been doing this prayer retreat for many years. The friend, Laurel who is hosting this event, said yes to my coming and said, "this may well be the last time you see each other". Kay's health isn't well. As I am in this valley of indecision, I realize I was looking forward to being with people that "knew me when," and I knew when. Old stories surfaced in my memories, fun, encouraging, and memorable answers to prayer. They made me smile.

My physical health card–am I going to be up to it to go? At my age, the reality is I take longer to recover from illness than it used to. It isn't a card that I used to give much value to–but not I have to. Will this card trump every other card in the hand? We will have to see.

Another card that surfaced was the desire to just spend time with the Lord in a new place with new people. Hearing their hearts and learning from them. Originally, there were going to be six of us. These are women who know their God and walk with Him. Their lives have not been easy. In fact, Laurel's husband has been in a coma for over a year, and is now in hospice care. She may not get to even attend the event (and I think I might be disappointed!) There are so many life lessons to be gleaned from these new and old friends. Both Kay and Malana have endured hard places, but they still choose to walk with Him. Both their spouses are still here, and I am sure my walk through the valley of death has helped them prepare, in case they find themselves alone. There is something special to be with those with whom you have history, and the Lord knows that.

The other disappointing card: My friends want me to come. It will be disappointing if I can't make it, it is part of the package of living life. I know they will understand. But it will make us all sad. It will have to be played if I don't feel better. Disappointing others is so hard for me. But I know the Lord will comfort their hearts, even as He will comfort mine.

Another major card in dealing with disappointment is perspective and attitude. I know this ties into the emotion card, but the choice is where am I going to put it? Do I have any other unresolved disappointments that this situation can be added to? Or am I able to look at my life, accept that these things happen and move on? Unresolved disappointment can turn into bitterness and that defiles many, as the scripture says. Not good for you or for others. Would this trip add wonderful memories, insights, and blessings to my life? Yes! But, if I can't make it, will it really harm me in the long run? Probably not. After all, I surrendered my life to the Lord a long time ago. His ways are higher than my ways. Other disappointments (like my husband's heart attack/stroke) were not so easy to discard. I chose not to put it in the bitterness pile for myself, my family and my Lord. I admit, some days it tried to sneak back to that pile! But friends, I encourage you to take the time to process every disappointment. For your spiritual, emotional and physical sake, it is worth it.

My perspective card is just that, my perspective. If I can't go, I will choose not to mope and be sad. I am so grateful they want me to come. Just taking the time to reflect on our memories is such a blessing. Are there other cards in the disappointment hand? At times, yes. Disappointment often is a revealer. It reveals where our hope has been placed. I find out how mature I am, or not! Do I really have self-control, or is it an area I need to keep growing? Have I learned to accept God's yes's as well as His no's?

We all encounter disappointments. It's just a reality we must accept. I am so glad the Holy Spirit helps us walk through every one if we let Him. In Luke 24, Jesus appeared to His disciples after they had walked through his death. He loved them, as He loves us, and wanted to reassure it was really Him that was raised from the dead. Disappointments come, but so does Jesus. Let us look to Him, knowing He walks with us through any dark valley we encounter. Whether or not I make it to the Prayer Retreat, I will be glad and rejoice with my God, knowing He understands.

Father, I ask You to help us learn to deal with our disappointments. Help us not to veer to the left or to the right; but to stay on course with You. Let me bring You into my disappointment, not blame You for it. In Jesus' Name, amen.

24.

Faith when Overwhelmed

*O God, listen to my cry! Hear my prayer! From the ends of the
earth, I cry to you for help when my heart is overwhelmed.
Lead me to the towering rock of safety, Psalm 61:1-2 (NLT)*

Phone calls, text messages, Facebook posts, emails, and even cards and letters can bring good news or bad news. Sometimes the bad news seems to roll in like a flood. How do we walk in faith when we feel overwhelmed?

Are you finding yourself feeling overwhelmed? I looked up the word. It means *to bury or drown beneath a huge mass, or be too strong for, overpower*! I admit I have walked through some of those days where I feel I'm drowning in a myriad of troubles. Remember Job, and all the bad news he received in one day? I imagine he was feeling overwhelmed. I have had days where I felt like I couldn't take a deep breath as the concerns of life flooded my soul. They were not as bad as Job's, but it felt like it!

King David wrote Psalm 61. If you are not familiar with his life's struggles, take time to read the books of 1 and 2 Samuel. This was a man who loved God but encountered his share of challenges in following him. David's example of crying out to the Lord when he was overwhelmed is something to emulate. We need to run to him, not sit in our distress. Know that he is a safe refuge even when we are feeling overwhelmed by life and its demands.

David was overwhelmed by his circumstances in this Psalm. We find that we can be overwhelmed by guilt, Psalm 38:4 or sin Psalm 65:3. If you find yourself overwhelmed by guilt you must take the time to discover whether it is real guilt or false guilt. False guilt and condemnation can follow us around like a dirty cloud until we take authority over it in Jesus' name and apply the blood of Jesus to the situation. It is the same with sin. If we are dealing with unconfessed sin, we need to get it right through repentance and trust in our salvation. There is no need to be barraged by our past. It is under the blood. You are free!

There is another description of being overwhelmed described in Isaiah 61:10 (NLT). *I am overwhelmed with joy in the Lord* my God! For he has dressed me with the clothing of salvation *and draped me in a robe of righteousness.* This is walking in the knowledge of exactly what our salvation has purchased us. Taking time to focus on God's great grace and mercy does produce an overwhelming joy and understanding that every-thing truly will be ok. The more we are overwhelmed by his goodness, the less we will be overwhelmed by our circumstances.

The Apostle Paul writes in 2 Corinthians 1:8-10 (NLT) about being overwhelmed as well. *We think you ought to know, dear brothers and sis-ters, about the trouble we went through in the province of Asia. We were crushed and overwhelmed beyond our ability to endure, and we thought we would never live through it. In fact, we expected to die. But as a result, we stopped relying on ourselves and learned to rely only on God, who raises the dead. And he did rescue us from mortal danger, and he will rescue us again. We have placed our confidence in him, and he will continue to rescue us.*

I can't imagine what Paul and all his co-laborers went through. When things are too big for us to handle, it forces us to turn to the Lord for his wisdom, resources, and supply. This is not a bad thing. Most of the time when we feel overwhelmed, we also feel out of control. When this happens remind yourself that God is never out of control, but has the situation in hand.

Paul's perspective is something we should strive for, the knowledge that God will rescue us in and through whatever would come and try to overwhelm us. The truth is they learned to stop relying on themselves and learned to rely only on God. This is the key to walking through overwhelming circumstances with faith; relying on the Lord. Whether your 'huge mess' is financial, emotional, physical, or relational, God is with you. Marriage issues, parenting struggles, job problems, etc. can all seem overwhelming at the time. Cry out to him, find his safe refuge, take a breath and discover the solutions you need.

Isn't it great how we can learn from biblical processes when feeling overwhelmed? I am so thankful for David's transparency and honesty about his emotions and feelings. It is not a sin to feel overwhelmed. *Psalm 61:1-3a (NLT) O God, listen to my cry! Hear my prayer! From the ends of the earth, I cry to you for help when my heart is overwhelmed. Lead me to the towering rock of safety, for you are my safe refuge,"*

Step 1: We are not alone in feeling overwhelmed. It is a part of life.

Step 2: Go to God. Cry out to him, ask for his help, and believe he will answer.

Step 3: Move to the safety of understanding his care and presence.

Step 4: Look for his solutions and tokens for his good. Remind yourself of his loving care.

Step 5: Start by handling something you can do.

Father, please help me look up when I am feeling overwhelmed. Remind me that you are with me, and I do not have to face any situation alone. Thank you for helping me hide in the rock of your safety and under your wonderful wings. Thank you for helping me grow during these times of testing and trials. I choose to trust you, dear Father.

In Jesus' Name, amen.

25.

Faith and the 'Why Me' Temptation

For you know that when your faith is tested,
your endurance has a chance to grow. James 1:3 (NLT)

One of Satan's tricky, but predictable tactics is some form of the 'why me's'? Why do I have to deal with this (fill in the blank for your own 'this'). We all have them. Some can be the biggies of life: the unexpected death of a loved one, diagnosis of chronic illness, or failed relationships. These major life challenges are difficult enough to process, without the added struggle of self-pity. As we look around and see others without our difficulties, we can fall into self-pity and complaints. The 'why me' syndrome arises and can take us down to the pits of despair. Sometimes these are so big that we desperately need the Lord's help to circumvent the 'why me's', and rush to 'Help Me, Lord'!

However, Satan's goal is to work with our minds and emotions to get our eyes off our God and onto ourselves. If he can't get us during the 'biggies' then he will try the 'smallies'. Things like a broken shoelace, lost keys, or misplaced cell phone can cause us to feel like the universe is against us, and that old familiar 'why me' syndrome can rear its whisper. Grumbles and mumbles suck our faith and joy, taking the place of gratitude and thankfulness. Thought by thought our faith wanes and unbelief, fear and discouragement try to take the reins and lead us away from God's hope and blessing. I believe we are all susceptible to this warfare tactic.

Why? Because it works! Another way the 'why me' assault works is by causing us to compare ourselves to others. The 'they' versus 'us' ploy comes into play. Why do they get a new car, a great vacation, or a promotion? In most cases it causes us to feel like we get the shorter end of the stick than others. 'They' are perceived to receive a better blessing, more honor, or protection against the difficult trials of life.

These thoughts are like mosquitos whining around our minds. If we capture them before we get bit, then we won't be dealing with the fallout of the itchiness. These itches detract us from what we are supposed to be thinking about like the yeses and blessings we have received. It takes discipline and spiritual sensitivity to follow 2 Corinthians 10:5 instruction to *take every thought captive to obey Christ.* As soon as you recognize these anti-faith thoughts of deadly comparison cast them down and replace them with God's word or if you can't think of an appropriate scripture at the time, then begin to remind yourself that you have a loving heavenly Father who cares for you.

Sometimes these attacks do not have anything to do with others. Instead, the whys cause us to doubt God's power, presence, and goodness in our life. Why did cancer hit our family? Why do I have to raise a child with disabilities? Why was I born into such a dysfunctional family? These are times when deliberately reminding yourself of God's character and faithfulness must come into play. As the Lord is your shepherd, trust him to lead you back to the still waters and quiet resting places. He will restore your soul from any warfare damage as you walk with him.

One of the scriptures that helped me walk through the initial stages of grief, when my husband suffered a stroke and later died may seem strange to you. Matthew 5: 44-45, *But I say to you, love your enemies and pray for those who persecute you, so that you may be sons of your Father who is in heaven. For he makes the sun rise on the evil and on the good and sends rain on the just and on the unjust.*

The rain falling on the just and the unjust reminded me during that time, that why not me? Why shouldn't I suffer as others have suffered? I began to pray, Father, please get every good you can from these difficult circumstances. Teach me, lead me, and guide me through these rough waters. Your word tells me when I walk *through the waters or through the fire* you will be with me.

I truly believe if we capture the 'why me' thoughts, God will teach us his ways and we will discover his purpose in both the biggies and the smallies of life. Let's keep on trusting him and not allow the 'why me' temptations to steal our joy or blessings. Sometimes the very things that we would want to ask the Lord why us, are the very things he has planned to use for his glory in our future. It all comes down to trusting him. We can do this!

Father, I am so glad for your mercy. I ask that you help us grow up and out of the why me, stage of life. Show us where we fall short in these areas, and give us eyes of faith to accept our specific struggles in life. Help us choose to trust you no matter what comes our way.

In Jesus' Name, amen.

26.

Faith Walking Challenges

The Lord has done it this very day; let us rejoice today and be glad.
Psalm 118:24 (NIV)

Some days are just made for steady walking. No great outward progress, but just a determination to walk in faith with what you know is true, right, and just. This is especially true when you are praying for, waiting for, or even longing for some outward change. It is sometimes difficult to 'keep the faith' during the silent times.

People have been waiting for answered prayer since time began! Abraham, Sarah, and Noah are great examples in the Old Testament. Then we find Mary and Martha in the New Testament. Mary and Martha waited anxiously for Jesus to return when Lazarus was ill. I can only imagine as they nursed him, watching him grow weaker and looking out the window, expectantly.

Is that him coming? Why isn't he here yet?

We don't hear of any messenger sending words of hope or regret from Jesus. Just silence.

I wonder if Mary and Martha reminded themselves of Jesus' other miracles, reassuring each other that surely he would arrive soon. After all, in their message, they said, *"Lord, your **dear friend** is very sick." John 11:3 (NLT).* Alas, he didn't arrive. Then Lazarus died. They had to face reality. He was dead. Without their miracle-working friend.

Immediately, Mary and Martha went about the burial preparations. I wonder if they did it slowly, giving Jesus a chance to show up. Preparing the spices, wrapping the body, and maybe even preparing the tomb to receive the body. Fulfilling the mandatory duties for Lazarus to be buried.

Maybe they were gaining strength from the story of the widow of Nain, who was on her way to bury her only son when a chance encounter with Jesus brought him alive once again. Still, there was no sign of Jesus. According to the custom of the day, they still needed to bury him on the day he died.

Friends and relatives were there to grieve with the sisters. Day two, no Jesus. Plenty of time to mourn and wonder where Jesus was. Do you think they might have even entertained thoughts such as, "we fed them a lot," "I thought he loved us," etc. By then, perhaps they had begun to accept the fact that their brother was gone. Day Four arrived, and *when Martha got word that Jesus was coming, she went to meet him. But Mary stayed in the house. John 11:20 (NLT).*

The focus here isn't about the raising of Lazarus necessarily, but to help us learn how to stay faith-filled during difficult, silent times. Martha declared her trust and faith in Jesus. She stated what she knew. "...*Lord, if only you had been here, my brother would not have died. But even now I know that God will give you whatever you ask."* Jesus told her, "Your *brother will rise again." "Yes," Martha said, "he will rise when everyone else rises, at the last day." John 11: 21-24*

It is important that during emotional times we begin to speak the truth we know, rather than focus on the mysteries of what we don't know. Even simple declarations of, "God, I know you love me, even in the midst of this situation", "I thank you for loving me through this," or "I trust you to bring me through." One of my go-to prayers is, "Lord, you know how extremely difficult this is, I ask that you get every good thing you can out of it!"

And we know that God causes everything to work together for the good of those who love God and are called according to his purpose for them." Romans 8:28 NLT

When Mary arrived and saw Jesus, she fell at his feet and said, "Lord, if only you had been here, my brother would not have died." She was honest in her response. This is the Mary that sat at Jesus' feet to learn from him, instead of serving with Martha. Perhaps it was those things she learned at his feet that kept her trusting him. Both sisters could have 'gone bitter' during his absence, but they did not go there. We need to guard our hearts and keep trusting his character.

Many times it may not be us experiencing direct grief or loss, but it may be our friends or family members. This story does not share their friend's thoughts or feelings, but we know they had them. Often it is hard to know how to support others during their difficult times. They did the right thing, they showed up! Never underestimate the power of showing up, it speaks volumes, gives hope, shows your care, and helps bring stability. Leave your unanswered questions at home, just show up and love your friends. I hope none of Martha and Mary's friends spent time discussing the fact that Jesus hadn't shown up earlier! Walking in faith means we need to acknowledge our feelings, but not let them rule our spirit. In seasons of grief and loss, it is extremely challenging to put this into practice. We can take comfort with Jesus' words to Martha. *Jesus told her, "I am the resurrection and the life. Anyone who believes in me will live, even after dying."* John 11:25 (NLT)

Challenging times often bring us to the place where we must answer that question, "Do you believe this?" If we discover the answer is, 'I am not sure,' don't be condemned. Take it as an opportunity to learn more about him and his thoughts in whatever area you are facing. The Teacher will come. What joy erupted when Jesus spoke those words, "Lazarus, come forth!" No matter what we go through, there is life afterward. God's promises are true and faithful. We can trust him during the quiet times. Psalm 23:4 (NLT) *declares, even when I walk through the darkest valley, I will not be afraid, for you are close beside me. Your rod and your staff protect and comfort me."*

Father, please help us trust you and walk in faith during challenging and difficult times. Thank you for being close to those who are grieving and feeling hopeless for any reason. Encourage their hearts to choose to trust that you will reveal yourself at the right time. Thank you that we do not have to walk in fear in our darkest valley, for you are with us.

In Jesus' Name, Amen

27.

Faith and the Why Question

For I know the plans I have for you," says the Lord. "They are plans for good and not for disaster, to give you a future and a hope.
Jeremiah 29:11(NLT)

How do we grapple with the questions that arise in our lives? The difficult circumstances of life often provoke some of the most challenging questions that can disrupt, disturb or disconnect our relationship with God or amazingly, cause us to draw closer to him.

Last week I received news that an old friend's teenage grandson passed away in his sleep. As of now, I don't know if they even have a medical reason. He just went to sleep and did not wake to another day on this earth. Reading his obituary it sounds like he touched many lives in his abbreviated time for which I am sure his family is so thankful. However, I am sure as they navigate life with this new hole, they are struggling with the question of why.

It has been many years since my husband's debilitating stroke and while my hole has become more bearable, it is still with me every day. My children still miss their father and for most of our grandchildren, grandpa is just another story told. I know he would have added such a wonderful dimension to their lives and I can only wonder, why.

I've learned that these types of questions don't produce much faith. Yes, they are real and must be grappled with, but as I've been walking single I have to choose not to focus on those types of questions. The type of questions that lead me forward are those that ask, "What now, Lord? What would you have me do now?"

Jesus is not afraid of our questions. In fact, he liked to ask questions. 307 of them are listed in the gospels! Most of them he didn't even bother answering. He just left them out there for the hearers to think about them. I think maybe he responds to my 'why's' in the same way, letting them hang in the air so my ears can hear their feeble cry, and understand the foolishness of them!

It is not that he doesn't care, it is just he has a time and place to reveal his purpose and plan. I'm beginning to see and rejoice in my new life. More compassion, more patience with others, and more openness to his servants leading are some of the fruits that I see in my own life. I'm glad I have more time to interact with my grandchildren and help lighten my children's parental load at times. I've come to understand God's love and acceptance for me on a much deeper level as I sought my new identity in him. These are all part of the things he has promised to work out for good in my life. I am so grateful for them.

I listened to a Facebook clip by Angelina Jolie posted on a friend's timeline. She had just received the Jean Hersholt Humanitarian award during the 2013 Academy Awards ceremony. During the acceptance speech, she wondered out loud, "I don't know why I was born and given the opportunities I was, while there sits another woman in a refugee camp with as much talent, drive, and energy as I have." (paraphrased) She ended with the encouragement to make the best use of the life we've been given. That is my desire. To make the best use of the life I have been given and to live with as much courage and trust as I can. If I were to concentrate on all the whys in my life, I should be asking why my children were born whole and healthy and some children are born with disabilities. Why did I enjoy a wonderful happy marriage, while others struggle with abuse and pain? Why were we adopted at eleven months old, while other children struggle with life in the foster care program?

Maybe instead of asking why me, Lord? I should be asking, why not me? Again, it comes down to a place of trust. Jeremiah 29:11 tells us, *"For I know the plans I have for you," says the Lord. "They are plans for good and not for disaster, to give you a future and a hope. In those days when you pray, I will listen. If you look for me wholeheartedly, you will find me. I will be found by you,..."* How encouraging to know that when I seek him, I will find him. His presence, peace, and purpose are revealed as I choose to walk with him. I could stand as a little kid and throw a temper tantrum, but that wouldn't change things. As I learn to accept my situation, both the good and the difficult, I see myself moving toward maturity. In the meantime, there are so many hurting people who need our love, compassion, and understanding. As I reach out to them, I become even more grateful for my own life. I realize, by the grace of God that when I focused on all the whys of my life; life itself was passing me by. I am grateful for his patience during my why stages and I am grateful for his leading me past them. Will I stumble back into them? Maybe! But he will once again lead me through the valley of the shadow of doubt and whys, a figurative aspect of death, isn't it?

Father, I ask you to help everyone find their way through their muddles of why and bring peace to every hurting soul. I thank you for the presence of your Holy Spirit to comfort, lead and direct us.

In Jesus' Name, amen.

28.

Faith and "Feelings"

Do nothing out of selfish ambition or vain conceit. Rather,
in humility value others above yourselves, not looking to your own
interests but each of you to the interests of the others.
Philippians 2:3-4 (NIV)

Our weather has been pretty cold and miserable here. One Sunday morning I woke up, all snuggled warm in my bed, thinking I don't really 'feel' like going to church this morning. I am not serving anywhere and the friend I pick up most Sundays didn't want to leave her house because of the snow. I was listening to the service from Living Word Fellowship, in Voluntown, CT. Their different elders were discussing the privilege of coming and belonging to a church versus feeling like it is a duty. It was so encouraging, but I almost missed the point by focusing on my feelings!

I admit my feelings almost won, but I encouraged myself in the Lord, made it to pre-service prayer, and was so grateful that I went. In God's providence, I connected with a new lady who is now a part of our

Life Group. As I reflected on this moment, I wondered how often our feelings direct our path, rather than the Lord.

Feelings are fleeting. They come and go. They focus us on ourselves and can make us so very short-sighted. Our culture has become a 'what about me?' culture. As I pondered staying in bed and watching our church service online, I realized the decision I made definitely was about me. If we are to become the salt and light God desires us to be, we must learn to submit our feelings to him and his ways. I'm sure Paul didn't feel like enduring the beatings, shipwrecks and imprisonments he writes about in 2 Corinthians 11:26, but he learned to endure them like a good soldier. Now we still benefit from his writings.

If we are to become the influencers God desires us to be, we must learn self-control. Self-control is the ability to stop yourself from doing what you feel like doing that isn't in your or others' best interest. Self-control is actually growing up. Toddlers react to their feelings immediately, as adults, we should be able to control those feelings. We mustn't act like little children, but we must mature in our thoughts and actions.

In Matthew 5, we find Jesus teaching about anger, adultery and divorce. The beginning of each of these actions started with a feeling which triggered an emotion that resulted in an action. I wonder how many divisions, divorces, and destructive actions begin with feelings. Feelings are not always based on fact, how much pain could or would be avoided if a person took the time to examine their feelings.

Feelings are God-given. God has them, but he uses them correctly. We must learn to submit them to the Lord, and use them correctly as well. He wants to teach us how. The ESV versions of Proverbs 16:32 states: *Whoever is slow to anger is better than the mighty, and he who rules his spirit than he who takes a city.*

Maybe anger isn't your struggle when dealing with feelings, but learning to rule your spirit when dealing with any feelings is important. Comparing the works of the flesh found in Galatians 5: 19-21 (ESV) *sexual immorality, impurity, sensuality, idolatry, sorcery, enmity, strife, jealousy, fits of anger, rivalries, dissensions, divisions, envy, drunkenness, orgies, and things like these* to the fruit of the spirit found in Galatians 5:22-23 (ESV) *love, joy, peace, patience, kindness, goodness, faithfulness, gentleness, self-control;* feelings are involved in both. When reading the works of the flesh list, I found it so destructive and something I do not want to encourage in my life.

Satan is looking for any foothold he can take in our lives. He isn't above using our feelings for his purposes. Philippians 2:3-8 (NIV) *Do nothing out of selfish ambition or vain conceit. Rather, in humility value others above yourselves, not looking to your own interests but each of you to the interests of the others. In your relationships with one another, have the same mindset as Christ Jesus: Who, being in very nature God, did not consider equality with God something to be used to his own advantage; rather, he made himself nothing by taking the very nature of a servant, being made in human likeness. And being found in appearance as a man, he humbled himself by becoming obedient to death—even death on a cross!*

Dear friends, let us keep our feelings in their rightful place. Acknowledge them, examine their source, but do not let them rule your life. Your feelings, if allowed to run things, will lead you to a self-centered and eventually selfish life. Your flesh may be happy, but your spirit will suffer.

Father, help us in this area. We need to understand how to balance our feelings and your ways. I thank you for pouring out grace to us as we explore this area. Teach us that your ways are the best, even if we do not feel like it.

In Jesus' Name, amen.

29.

Faith and Developing Integrity

So he shepherded them according to the integrity of his heart, And guided them by the skillfulness of his hands. Psalm 78:72 NKJV

God prepared David and took this gentle shepherd-king and presented him before the people as the one who would love and care for them with integrity, a pure heart, and the anointing to lead Israel, his holy inheritance. Psalm 78:71-72 TPT

Do we even think about the importance of integrity in our everyday life? Probably not until something or someone lets you down does it even cross your mind. The Passion Translation expands in verse 72 and makes it clear that the qualities David had as a leader were integrity, a pure heart, and the anointing. As I read these scriptures, I realized that integrity is something that is only in our own control. Conviction of the Holy Spirit and our conscience can help remind us to live with integrity, but in reality, the choice is up to us. My integrity is just that, my integrity. Integrity is the quality of being honest and having strong moral principles. A person with integrity always seeks to reflect their ethical standards regardless of circumstance. It is something each person must develop within themselves. A person without integrity has no internal boundaries or borders when temptation, tests, and trials arise. The quality of integrity shows up during the challenges of life. How will we respond? It is something we all want others to have in their relationship with us! Many scriptures talk about not only the blessing of integrity but also the problems of those who live dishonestly.

Better is a poor person who walks in his integrity than one who is crooked in speech and is a fool. Proverbs 19:1 (ESV)

Whoever walks in integrity walks securely, but he who makes his ways crooked will be found out. Proverbs 10:9 (ESV)

The righteous who walks in his integrity—blessed are his children after him! Proverbs 20:7(ESV)

Reading these scriptures, it seems obvious that everyone would choose to walk with integrity, right? However, we know this is not the case. Remember when Peter vowed he would never betray Jesus, and of course, he did. Fear caused Peter to break his vow, but the good news is we see God's grace, mercy, and anointing, strengthening Peter to the point he was martyred for his faith.

In 2 Kings 5, we find the amazing story of Naaman, a commander of the army of Syria. He had leprosy and God connected him with the prophet Elisha. Naaman obeyed Elisha's instructions and was healed. Naturally, he was grateful and wanted to give gifts to Elisha in gratitude, but Elisha said no. Unfortunately, Gehazi, Elisha's servant greedily went to him, lied, and asked for the forbidden gifts. His greed overcame his loyalty and showed his lack of integrity. Elisha called him out, and he went from

Elisha's presence as a leper. As a leper, he could no longer be the prophet's servant. He missed out on being part of some amazing miracles.

As believers, people expect us to walk in honesty, tell the truth, and be people of our word. Sadly, due to fear, like Peter, or greed like Gehazi, our flesh often dictates our actions. So how do we grow in our integrity? First, by identifying what your core values are. The ones you refuse to compromise on. Find out where fear or greed may be areas of temptation and build up those walls. I believe as David worshipped God, God grew bigger and more real to him, which allowed him to honor the things God honors. When he could have killed King Saul, David chose not to. He was a man of integrity. When he messed up, he owned it. A man of integrity does not have to be a perfect person, but he needs to own up to his mistakes. Gehazi, when found out, tried to cover up his actions.

This week, I admit, I dealt with two situations where integrity was breached. One was with a lawyer, the other at a medical clinic. I am trusting the Lord to work through each circumstance, which is out of my control and see him bring good from them. I don't think either of them deliberately set out to dishearten me, but they did. So my choice is to forgive and walk on. I don't want to be a stone thrower of accusations or set myself up as an example of the only integral person around because I am not. I can choose to do my best to be a woman of integrity, relying on the Holy Spirit's help. With a fresh understanding of how important it is to others for me to keep my word, I walk on, being quick to forgive.

Father, I ask you to help us in this area. I know we all want others to walk integrity toward us, but we need your help to do the same. Thank you for the promises we read in your word that come from walking in integrity. Fear and greed are two major areas where your people stumble. Please show us any place where our walls are down. As we grow in our trust in you fear and greed will not have such a hold on us. Forgive us when we fall short, help us make it right.

In Jesus' Nam, amen.

30.
Faith and Stirring UP!

This is why I remind you to fan into flames the spiritual gift
God gave you when I laid my hands on you.
2 Timothy 1:6 (NLT)

"Fan into flames the spiritual gift God gave you," Paul
wrote to his dear son, Timothy. The NIV translation exhorts
him to, *"stir up the gift of God which is in you."* A spiritual gift is given to each of us so we can help each other.
1 Corinthians12:7 (NLT)

Somebody else needs you to use your gifts.

A few weeks ago my power went out. Fortunately, I have a wood
stove insert as an alternate heating source. I have been saving some wood
for just this scenario, but then I struggled to get the fire going. Starting
fires from scratch can be difficult. My paper source was limited so it took
me quite a while to get that fire going. I had tiny matches, which with

the draft from the stove kept blowing out before I got to the paper! I was determined to get the fire going so I could have heat in the house and a place to boil water for my coffee!

In our earlier married life, my husband and I lived in several places where we used wood stoves as our primary heat source. The difference between then and now, besides the fact that he was usually the fire starter, was that we kept the fired 'banked' at night. There were usually coals that with a little encouragement or fanning, the fire would quickly catch the new logs on the fire. Paul's encouragement to Timothy to, "stir up the gift of God which is in him," speaks strongly to us today. Have the circumstances of your life caused you to let your gifts go dormant? These gifts can range from all of the spiritual gifts listed in Romans 12 or 1 Corinthians 12. The gifts of encouragement, exhortation, and comfort are so needed these days.

Stirring and fanning are very deliberate actions. We as individuals are to stir up or fan our flames. How do we do that? First, we must believe there is a good gift that needs to be stirred. If your fire has gone out or dwindled to almost nothing, please know your gifts are important to those around you. Take time to pray, asking the Lord to bring his truth to the situation - it is vital. Satan would love for your fire to go out completely, for your influence to be shut down and for the help it brings to others to be thwarted. I say it again, your gift is important.

Your words of encouragement and caring may be the very thing that spurs another on to stir up their gift. Natural fires go out if the logs are separated. Spiritual life also diminishes if we try to do life alone. Timothy needed Paul's encouragement. We need to encourage others to keep burning bright. Stir up any dormant gifts you have been keeping in reserve. Activate them and see what God will do in and through you.

Father, I thank you for stirring up the flame that lies within each of your children. I ask you to help us understand that every gift you have given us is important to use for your Kingdom's sake. Teach us how to keep the flames kindled and going.

In Jesus' Name, amen.

31.

Faith and the All-Purpose Gift

Do nothing out of selfish ambition or vain conceit. Rather,
in humility value others above yourselves, not looking to your own
interests but each of you to the interests of the others. Philippians
2:3-4 (NIV)

What is one thing that you could give everyone you meet? Old friends, new friends, ancient friends, young friends—happy friends or sad friends? This gift never expires, never goes out of usefulness. It doesn't take up shelf space, nor does it go bad and fill up the landfill. The package can be as unique as the person. This gift can change lives. Without it, many wither but with it most flourish. What is this amazing gift?

It is the gift of encouragement. The interesting thing about the gift of encouragement is that it turns our eyes from ourselves and onto others. Learning to become an encourager seems to be easier for some than for others. The good news is that everyone can become an encourager. It is a powerful gift that helps in our family life, our work life, and the kingdom life.

Encouragement gives us the energy to complete a task or objective. It can help change our perspective about ourselves and others. It can help restore our self-confidence when we are beginning to doubt ourselves. I read a story yesterday about a man who stopped by a McDonald's for the first time during Covid. As he paid for his order he noticed the young man's wrists had several cuts. When the young man handed him his order he began to speak encouragement to him. This gentleman was so burdened by this young man's condition he pulled over into the parking space and began to pray for him. A few minutes later the young man ran over to his car and thanked him. He said it was the first words of hope he had been given in four years. He felt seen. He felt heard and he gave his life to Jesus that day. The power of encouragement is real.

To use this gift to its full potential we need to turn our focus outward. We can't stay selfish or self-oriented, we must become people-centric. Jesus always looked outward. I believe the Holy Spirit will help us become more sensitive to the needs of others as we ask him to help us have eyes to see. We will become aware of body language, nuances in tones of voice, or word choices that will clue us in on others needing encouragement. We must slow down and become better listeners.

Why do we struggle in this area? Sometimes we don't know what to say. Sometimes we may judge that the person already knows that they are doing a good job, so why would they need us to affirm them? Maybe we are afraid they will become prideful. I have found that words of encouragement, when given from a sincere heart are never inappropriate. There is a difference between flattery and encouragement. Encouragement is given to build up the other person, flattery is given to get something from the other person. Checking our motives helps us stay on track. We must give this gift from a heart of love and compassion with sincerity, humility, and honesty.

Parents, acknowledge when your children are doing things right—especially those whose love language is words of affirmation. Be patient when they are learning something new. Encourage those small steps. Spouses encourage each other when you are struggling as a couple—we will get through this. Come on teammate, we can do this!

Choosing to be encouraging during times of strife, instead of accusing takes definite willpower and restraint, but it can yield much better fruit. If you remember words are like seeds and they grow what you plant, it is easier at times to plant words of encouragement versus words of discouragement.

For those of us who use Social Media—take the time to post a comment on somebody's post that is encouraging to you. Ask the Lord to show you who to encourage this week, leave a note on their page. Encourage your Pastor and leaders, your boss, your wife, or your husband with something good you noticed about them. Speak words of life to your children to help them through this struggling time.

Father, teach us to look after the concerns of others. Help us to become encouragers of our family, friends, brothers, and sisters in the Lord. Let genuine love become our highest goal—to love you and others.

In Jesus' Name, amen.

32.

Faith and Persistent Prayer

I waited patiently for the Lord to help me, and he turned to me and heard my cry. He lifted me out of the pit of despair, out of the mud and the mire. He set my feet on solid ground and steadied me as I walked along. Psalm 40:1-2 (NLT)

Last week our church scheduled a 'Seek Week'. It led up to our Vision Sunday where our Pastor reviewed last year and encouraged us with the vision for the year to come. Our leaders encouraged us to take time to fast and pray, not only for our church but also for our individual instructions or vision from the Lord. I will confess, due to many reasons this was one of the hardest times of fasting and prayer I have experienced.

As I did my best to set more time aside to seek the Lord I found I had to discipline myself to keep focused on the task at hand. I know there is a blessing in corporate prayer and a blessing in simple obedience to the fact that we were asked to participate, but still, I found resistance. Looking back, it was easier when Darryl and I would do it together, encouraging each other. I found I had to encourage myself in the Lord in some new ways! It's not that I haven't done it since he's been gone, it was just harder this time. I think maybe there was a grief aspect I hadn't anticipated. I am thankful for past testimonies of God's faithfulness when I have prayed and fasted. I kept reminding myself that it would be worth it when I finished it!

One night, I put on some worship music, opened a book I was reading called Dangerous Prayers by Pastor Craig Groeschel, and began to push through. The amazing thing was the Holy Spirit showed up. I opened my Bible to the scripture Pastor Groeschel was referencing and I slowly considered the words. It was a very special one-on-one experience with our Heavenly Father. I re-learned the lesson that slowing down with the Word can be so precious. There is no need to rush, when we slowdown is when we find the nuggets of truth that can sustain us through difficulties, humble us when we may be tempted to be prideful, and help us maintain our walk with him during this season on earth.

One scripture particularly stood out to me. *I Peter 5:10 (NLT) In his kindness God called you to share in his eternal glory by means of Christ Jesus. So after you have suffered a little while, he will restore, support, and strengthen you, and he will place you on a firm foundation.* Isn't that so comforting? He will restore, support and strengthen me after I suffer a little while. Persistent prayer during our times of suffering helps us stay the course. We find a similar word of encouragement in Psalm 40:1-3.

Psalm 40:1 (NIV) I waited patiently for the Lord; he turned to me and heard my cry. He lifted me out of the slimy pit, out of the mud and mire; he set my feet on a rock and gave me a firm place to stand. He put a new song in my mouth, a hymn of praise to our God. Many will see and fear the Lord and put their trust in him. Taking time to wait for him to show up, is not always easy. What a wonderful testimony David gave us, *"and He turned to me and heard MY cry."* David was in a very difficult place, but as he waited for the Lord, God brought him out and set his feet on his rock, and established his steps.

He does the same for us. He will establish our going. He will take away the song of lament and whining and replace it with a new song. A song that will cause praise to our God and this is the amazing part: *"Many will see it, and fear and will trust in the Lord!"* It is always encouraging to know that what I go through, as I do it with the Lord, will always bring help and hope to others. It is not just about me!

I have been praying big prayers for family and friends. I believe God is going to show up strong and bring hope and help even with some long-term stubborn situations. The key point is to wait patiently and in faith for our God to move. Releasing our faith while we pray and then resting in him works not only for ourselves but for others. Keep on asking, believing, and allowing him to change you and if necessary to help customize those prayers as needed. What an amazing God we serve. He does move mountains that seem to be stubborn against our prayers, we may feel as if we are moving them a spoonful at a time, but so be it! We do our part and God does his.

Father, encourage us to wait on you as we are praying. I speak encouragement to everyone who is tempted to quit. Help everyone to keep on running their race. Remember, he is working on your behalf even now. Father, send a token for good. I speak hope to the hopeless today. We look up in faith for the moving of your hand, your love is always towards us.

In Jesus' Name, Amen.

33.

Faith and Memory Stones

For this reason I remind you to kindle afresh the gift of God which is in you through the laying on of my hands. 2 Timothy 1:6 (NASB)

How's your memory? As we get older, we have so many more memories than we had when we were young. I remember standing at the marriage altar trying to capture in my memory the feelings and atmosphere of that special day. The same with the birth of each of our children, my first glimpse of each of their faces and the sense of new life and new stories being written for our family. I thought I would never forget, but sadly I do. As time goes by, those special feelings and memories begin to fade. One year I wrote their birth stories and gave it to each of my children so they would know how much we anticipated them and how they came into this world with a special opening chapter—written and planned by God, interwoven by my husband and me.

After forty years of wandering the wilderness, it finally came time for the children of Israel to enter the land promised by the Lord. Joshua 3:15-16 (NLT) tells us, *"It was the harvest season, and the Jordan was overflowing its banks. But as soon as the feet of the priests who were carrying the Ark touched the water at the river's edge, the water above that point began backing up a great distance away at a town called Adam, which is near Zarethan. And the water below that point flowed on to the Dead Sea until the riverbed was dry. Then all the people crossed over near the town of Jericho."*

How amazing would it be to be part of that amazing story? It would be one you think you could never forget, right? To watch the river dry up and watch God miraculously make a way where there really was no way! However, the Lord instructed Joshua to have the priests take up twelve stones from the river bed and make a memorial. We continue on in verse 21, *Then Joshua said to the Israelite, In the future your children will ask, "what do these stones mean?" Then you can tell them. This is where the Israelites crossed the Jordan on dry ground. For the Lord, your God dried up the river right before your eyes, and he kept it dry until you were all across, just as we did at the Red Sea when he dried it up until we had all crossed over. He did this so all the nations of the earth might know that the Lord's hand is powerful, and so you might fear the Lord your God forever.*

So I ask you to consider today...what are YOUR memorial stones? Do we mark the answered prayers in our life so we won't forget? Revelation tells us we overcome by the blood of the Lamb and the word of our testimony. My mom kept a diary for most of her life. She recorded moments in time that were important to her. Some are kind of boring to read but read as a larger picture gives us a glimpse into the many chapters of her life. I am grateful for them. Off and on in my life, I have kept a journal. Several years ago Darryl and I made a trip to Ghana and it was a memorable trip in so many ways, but re-reading my journal of that time I realize just how much God did in and through us! My conscious memory has lost those stories, but they are still available because I wrote them down.

Jesus told us to partake of the Lord's Supper as a memorial to him, *"this do in remembrance of me."* Why, because he knew we would forget. We need to be reminded of his death and sacrifice. He gave us a specific way to do this. We are asked to remember his body that was broken for us and his blood which was poured out for us. The elements of the bread and wine are our memorial stones, reminding us that we have a Savior who loves us. No matter how easy or difficult life may seem at communion time, it brings us back to the basics. We were sinners who needed a savior, and we have ONE!

I would encourage you to make your own memorial stones, these are not idols to be worshiped but simple reminders of how good your God has been at answering prayer, faithfully showing up, and showing forth His love to you and your family. During difficult times, it will serve to jog your memory and cause you to look up.

Father, I thank you for the gift of remembrance. I ask that you help us to remember the things we need to remember and forget those things we need to forget. Thank you for leaving us the Lord's Supper as a reminder of your work on the cross for us.

In Jesus' Name, amen.

34.
Faith and Celebrations!

*And on that day you will say, "Give thanks to the Lord, call
on His name. Make known His deeds among the peoples;
Make them remember that His name is exalted." Praise the Lord in
song, for He has done glorious things; Let this be known throughout the earth. Isaiah 12:4-5 NASB*

When you think of the Christian life, do you see it as a steady battle or a series of battles that seem never-ending? Sometimes it can feel like that. We can feel like Elisha's servant, who when faced with enemies all around felt hopeless and defeated. Elisha prayed, "Lord open his eyes," and he saw the angels of the Lord surrounding them. Victory came to them that day, and I am sure the servant was never the same. 2 Kings 6:16 Do you think they took the time to celebrate? I imagine they did.

Victories do come. One day, our daughter and her family experienced answered prayer in the selling of their rental home. Some people were saying No, but God said Yes. He sent them help from unexpected places and the sale closed. This was a major blessing and testimony, not only financially for their family, but also spiritually and emotionally. It is time to make a memorial stone of God's provision and intervention for future battles. It is time to rejoice and celebrate. How often do we experience answers to prayer and simply move on to requesting more needs be met without letting the victory of the moment impact our soul?

When the children of Israel crossed over the Jordan River into the Promised Land, the Lord told them to gather twelve stones, one for each tribe, and build a memorial as a reminder of God's faithfulness and strength. I believe it is a blessing for us to do the same.

What are some ways we can commemorate these victories?

First of all, take time to be grateful and thankful to the Lord.

Second, share the story! Tell people your victory story. Don't let Satan's lies rob you of this blessing to help strengthen your brother's and sister's walk; or miss out on the blessing of letting those that haven't heard of your God, hear his story in your life!

Third, journal it! Write it down. Date it. Your story doesn't have to be majorly significant to be written down. Sometimes the smallest stories bring the biggest impact. The act of writing it down will help cement it into your life. You will have a record to review during other difficult times.

Fourth: Do something special if you can. It doesn't have to be big, but let it be meaningful. While Elizabeth and Tim were signing papers, I bought donut holes for the kids to help celebrate God's answer to prayer for their family. We got donut holes because sugar isn't always their friend while they are in their Home Connection classes, but it made the day a little sweeter.

My other daughter and her family have been dealing with some serious battles for the past few months. It did my heart glad to hear their story! The parents snuck up on the kids and battled them with an unexpected silly string war as they were playing outside. They will never forget their parents attacking them with fun! The battle isn't over as yet, but hope and joy are part of the victory. Experiencing peace in the midst of storms is also part of God's gift and we can and should celebrate this gift as well.

I believe as we learn to celebrate EVERY victory, we will experience even more. We serve a faithful God who does answer prayer. The scripture says we have not because we ask not. Make sure you are asking for those victories you need!

Father, I thank you for your victories. I ask you to help us learn to celebrate the victories in our lives, this very day. I thank you for opening our eyes to them if we can't see them.

In Jesus' Name, amen.